Mumbai Post 26/11

Mumbai Post 26/11

An Alternate Perspective

Edited by
Ram Puniyani
Shabnam Hashmi

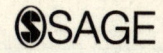

$SAGE www.sagepublications.com
Los Angeles • London • New Delhi • Singapore • Washington DC

Copyright © Ram Puniyani and Shabnam Hashmi, 2010

All rights reserved. No part of this book may be reproduced or utilized in any form or by any means, electronic or mechanical, including photocopying, recording or by any information storage or retrieval system, without permission in writing from the publisher.

First published in 2010 by

SAGE Publications India Pvt Ltd
B1/I-1 Mohan Cooperative Industrial Area
Mathura Road, New Delhi 110 044, India
www.sagepub.in

SAGE Publications Inc
2455 Teller Road
Thousand Oaks, California 91320, USA

SAGE Publications Ltd
1 Oliver's Yard, 55 City Road
London EC1Y 1SP, United Kingdom

SAGE Publications Asia-Pacific Pte Ltd
33 Pekin Street
#02-01 Far East Square
Singapore 048763

Published by Vivek Mehra for SAGE Publications India Pvt Ltd, typeset in 10.5/12.6pt Bembo by Star Compugraphics Private Limited, Delhi and printed at Chaman Enterprises, New Delhi.

Library of Congress Cataloging-in-Publication Data

Mumbai post 26/11: an alternate perspective/edited by Ram Puniyani and Shabnam Hashmi.
  p. cm.
  Includes bibliographical references.
  1. Terrorism—India—Bombay. 2. Terrorism—Prevention—India. I. Puniyani, Ram. II. Hashmi, Shabnam.

HV6433.I4M86   363.3250954'792—dc22   2009   2009047618

ISBN: 978-81-321-0308-0 (HB)

The SAGE Team: Rekha Natarajan, Meena Chakravorty, Vijay Sah and Trinankur Banerjee

Contents

Preface vii
Introduction xi

1. Terror: The Aftermath 1
   Anand Patwardhan
2. As the Fires Die: The Terror of the Aftermath 8
   Biju Mathew
3. Hotel Taj: Icon of Whose India? 16
   Gnani Sankaran
4. Why the United States Got it Wrong 23
   P. Sainath
5. Death of a Salesman 29
   Tarun Tejpal
6. Counter-terrorism Must not Kill Democracy 36
   Praful Bidwai
7. Responding to Mumbai Terror: Need for Diplomacy and Restraint, not War 43
   Praful Bidwai
8. Mumbai under Siege 50
   Yoginder Sikand
9. Handling Queries: Democratic Responses—Antulay Remarks and the Aftermath 59
   Ram Puniyani

10. The Mumbai Terror Attacks: Need for a Thorough Investigation ... 64
    Raveena Hansa

11. India's Terror Dossier: Further Evidence of Conspiracy ... 80
    Raveena Hansa

12. Terrorism, Rule of Law and Human Rights ... 97
    K.G. Balakrishnan

13. Acts of Terror and Terrorizing Act: Unfolding Indian Tragedy ... 104
    Sukla Sen

14. Our Politicians are Still not Listening ... 113
    Colin Gonsalves

15. Terrorism: Are Stronger Laws the Answer? ... 117
    Prashant Bhushan

16. Lessons from the Mumbai Attack ... 125
    Gautam Navlakha

Epilogue ... 138
Appendix I
   Acts of Terrorism by RSS Combine ... 142
Appendix II
   Unraveling Truth: People's Tribunal on Atrocities Committed in the Name of Combating Terrorism ... 145
Select Bibliography ... 150
About the Editors and Contributors ... 152

Preface

The attack on Mumbai (26 November 2008) came as a big jolt to the nation as a whole. Mumbai has been suffering from terrorist attacks earlier also, the major amongst them being the ones of 1993 and 2002. There have been other ones also, which shook the city and created a deep sense of insecurity. The one on 26 November 2008 was marked by a number of flaws in the security; the command structure for fighting against terror came to the light in a painful way. The vulnerability of citizens in the face of global and local atmosphere of terror was there for all to see. Close to 10 terrorists, well equipped with arms, armed to the teeth, land up on the Mumbai shore in a cool manner, take positions in strategic preplanned places, run amok around and maim innocent Mumbai citizens.

The control mechanism took a long time to be put in place. The local police, the military, the navy and finally the National Security Guards (NSG) took charge of the things to salvage the situation. There was a continuous television relay of the activities of terrorists, some of which they watched themselves, the fear and tragedy mix-up and create all the confusions to intensify terrorizing atmosphere.

The average citizen feels frustrated and helpless once again—helpless in the face of unexpected political tragedy, which is not easy to combat and helpless against the inefficient control mechanisms which are hardly in place. Since India in general and Mumbai in particular has faced many acts of terror, the angst is much more intense. And this time around the problem is also of a different magnitude, the terrorists flaunt their indoctrinated mind to land up in an alien country with the aim of killing innocent people, on the pretext of revenge of things which are delineated along communal lines. The worst part of the whole tragedy is that a few brilliant and efficient police officers were also killed in the insane act which was going on.

Such a terrible phenomenon drew many responses. There was a huge coverage of the incident and an equally elaborate analysis of the tragedy. The initial response of helpless citizens was to express their anger against the politicians as a class, perceiving that it is they who should be in charge; it is they who have failed the country and the city. In the process, the Union Home Minister, the Maharashtra Chief Minister and Deputy Chief Minister had to put in their papers. The central government brought in new legislations, with the hope that the legislation will help in preventing the future acts of terror. At another level it was decided that NSG will be posted not just in Delhi but in other major cities and places where the threat is perceived. The security at stations, airports was further strengthened.

Pakistan was confronted with the evidence that the terrorists came from there, and Pakistan government is answerable for these acts, irrespective of the fact whether the perpetrators are state or non-state actors, so far as these acts originate from there. It is not just that since they were not being encouraged by Pakistan government, this fact exonerates them from the blame of this act. Fortunately the talk of avenging the attack on Mumbai by retaliating and attacking Pakistan, as it emerged, died down soon enough and the government took the path of reasoned approach to the issue rather than succumbing to the emotional hysterical atmosphere which prevailed in the country for the time being. Mercifully since that episode similar terrorist groups have been active but not in India but in Pakistan itself. Day in and day out Pakistan is facing the problem and that too at a much worse level. The Taliban took possession of Swat valley and unleashed their fundamentalist agenda there—atrocities on innocent citizens, targeting of minorities in particular.

This 26/11 attack raised multiple questions: the questions related to the nature of terrorism itself, the peculiarities of this attack, the political repercussions and responses which followed and the change in the security atmosphere here. Many a valuable articles appeared in the media, which also went deeper and tried to analyze as to what is the nature of attack, how do we look at it and what are the discrepancies in the versions of the tragedy as presented in the media, etc. We also took up the articles critiquing the legislations and what lessons can be learnt from this whole episode.

In the surcharged atmosphere of South Asia such incidents do not only bring in massive tragedies but also have adverse impact on political milieu. It is in this light that we decided to put together these thought provoking contributions for this volume. Editors are grateful to Mansi Dev for her invaluable help. We do thank all the contributors of this volume and also Rekha Natarajan of SAGE for giving valuable feedback for introduction to the book.

March 2009 **Ram Puniyani**
Shabnam Hashmi

Introduction

Mumbai has been a victim of acts of terror from last several years. To be more precise, the first major one occurred on 12 March 1993, in which 13 blasts took place across the city killing 257 people. These were the blasts which took place in the aftermath of post-Babri demolition carnage. Later, Mumbai also witnessed the acts of terror on 2 December 2002 when an explosion took place in a bus in Ghatkopar suburb of Mumbai killing two people. The backdrop to this was the massive anti-Muslim pogrom in the wake of Godhra train burning. Similar tragedy shook the city on 13 March 2003, 29 July 2003, 25 August 2003 and the last one on 11 July 2006, in the Ist class compartment of Western Railway local trains.

The one on 26 November 2008 was of a different nature. It was an operation planned meticulously by a group of jeans and T-shirt wearing terrorists numbering nearly 10. It seems that they hijacked a Gujarat-registered fishing vessel on the high seas, sailed near Sassoon docks and reached the Gateway of India in dinghies. They were carrying heavy backpacks; and divided themselves into five teams and unleashed mayhem mainly at CST, G.T. Hospital, Metro Cinema, Hotel Taj, Hotel Trident and Nariman House. The blasts took place at these places and also at Colaba market, Cama Hospital, Nehru Road (Vile Parle), NB Road (Malad) and at Free Press Road. The attack literally took the breath of Mumbai away for a while, '[…] scale audacity, flamboyance and planning of this assault takes one's breath away. As the faces of anonymous, but not hooded, assassins flashed on TV screens, one thing became quickly clear. And what a spectacular success from their perspective, the operation has been' (Mehta, 2008). It seems that a lot of preparation had gone in to plan this attack, 'Mumbai attackers had clearly been trained well; the conspiracy had been in the making for close to a year; 10 of the 32 who had been trained were handpicked for Mission Mumbai and the planning was as detailed as lethal' (Baweja, 2009).

The attack left 126 people—98 civilians, 14 policemen and 14 foreigners—dead and 327 injured. The response, the combat against the terror attack was a very confused affair which is a matter of great concern. One example gives a good idea of the efficacy of the response, 'the Commandos arrived at Taj (Hotel) but declared, in the finest traditions of Indian bureaucracy, that they would not enter the hotel unless they received a written request from the Maharashtra Government' (Sanghavi, 2009). The Maharashtra Anti Terrorism Squad Chief Hemant Karkare, who was investigating Malegon blasts, was also killed in this episode of violence, along with other top police officials Ashok Kamte and Vijay Salaskar. The Maharashtra government appointed Ram Pradhan Committee to look at the role of police in defending the city. The committee released its report on 26 May 2009. The report has not been made public so far but as per media reports the report overall exonerates police machinery from any severe shortcomings.

I

Terrorism is a phenomenon which has been tormenting the world from last couple of decades. At the global level, the formation of Al Qaeda triggered this phenomenon. In India it was the post-Babri-violence, bomb blasts in Mumbai, which drew attention to this phenomenon. At the world level, the World Trade Center attack on 9/11, 2001, leaving nearly 3,000 dead, was the event which drew global attention to acts of terror.

As such it is not easy to define the word terrorism. The broad contours of the definition should include killings of non-combatants, a political motive or a statement behind that and the secret planning where the actors are willing or keen to lay down their lives (Hensman, 2002). Terrorist acts can also be done by those groups who are fighting for their rights with their backs to the wall in the face of intense oppression. The latter are in the areas where ethno-national issues are to the fore. Examples of this are Ireland, Kashmir, North East India and Tamils in Jaffna (Sri Lanka). While the definition of terrorism eludes an easy formulation, the acts of terror can easily be identified.

Terrorism is a very old phenomenon. During the 20th century it came to the fore after the Second World War. With the formation of Israel and many new nation-states, one sees acts of terror beginning at different places. With the exile of 14 lakh (lakh is hundred thousand) Palestinians from their home and hearth, the world saw the emergence of this phenomenon in that region. Then similar acts were seen around Irish question and Kashmir question. The identity and material concerns in North East India and Sri Lanka's Jaffna witnessed the emergence of terror groups, in different names, the major of which, Liberation Tigers of Tamil Elam, has recently been vanquished at a very heavy price of lives of thousands of innocent Tamil civilians. Here the primary identity of terror groups has not been drawn from a religion but primarily the area, ethnicity. As such, religious identity has been used for terrorism from the last two decades of the 20th century. Khalistani movement, which began in Punjab leading to Operation Blue Star, did it partly. One recalls the trajectory of events leading to the Indira Gandhi assasination by the Khalistanis.

Later the identity of religions was fully exploited for political goals of various political players in the world. Terrorism with the 'religious label' has been a phenomenon taking centre stage from the decade of 1990s. Arundhati Roy (2002) in *Algebra of Infinite Justice* points out,

In 1979, after the Soviet invasion of Afghanistan, the CIA and Pakistan's ISI (Inter Service Intelligence of the Pakistan Army) launched the largest covert operation in the history of CIA. Their purpose was to harness the energy of Afghan resistance to the Soviets, and expand it into a holy war, an Islamic Jihad, which would turn the Muslim countries within the Soviet zone of influence, against the communist regime and to eventually destabilize it. When it began, it was meant to be Soviet Union's Vietnam. It turned out to be much larger than that. Over the years,

CIA funded and recruited 100,000 radical Mujahidin from 40 Islamic countries as soldiers for American proxy war (in Afghanistan). (Roy, 2002)

Ninan Koshy (2002) says,

[…] the war against Afghans was very much in line with the US' historical role in Afghanistan. In the 1970s, the US hired seven different parties of fundamentalists called 'Mujahidin'. These were extremists hired by the CIA during the Cold War 'to draw the Soviets into Afghan trap', as later revealed by former National Security Advisor, Zbignew Brezinsky. The CIA gave arms and ammunition to these 'Mujahidin' […] Using these weapons and sophisticated training in the art of terror, these men successfully drove out the Soviets, but also waged terrible war on their own people killing at least 45,000 people in Kabul alone.

The Reagan regime went on for a proxy war. 'Built on Nixon doctrine—"Asian boys must fight Asian wars"—as applied by Henry Kissinger, its effect was to redesign American war strategy. Instead of a possible confrontation with Soviet ground troops in Europe, it prepared to wage low intensity conflict against militant nationalist regimes of third world' (Mamdani, 2005). In 1985, while introducing the visiting radical Islamists, Ronald Regan declared in the press conference, 'These gentlemen are the moral equivalents of America's founding fathers.' Politics was given the garb of religion and the whole world politics was vitiated due to the US machinations.

From here Al Qaeda came up. Osama bin Laden, a Saudi civil engineer, came to lead it. Mamdani points out that US pumped 8,000 million dollars to train these Mujahidins and gave 7,000 tonnes of armaments, including Stringer Missiles. With this formidable support the Al Qaeda joined the forces against the Soviet Army. The Soviet army was defeated in due course. Later the same Al Qaeda turned its jihad against US and India in Kashmir. Same elements are involved in a big way currently in operation in Pakistan (beginning part of 2009), the result of which has been not only multiple acts of terror—attack on Hotel Marriot, the murder of ex-Prime Minister Benazir Bhutto—but also the control in Swat valley and a threat to overthrow the nascent democracy in Pakistan. Most of the Pakistani leaders, the elected ones, have pointed out these facts in many of their articles and speeches.

With 9/11, the cycle turned the full circle and George W. Bush declared the War on terror. He went on to declare, 'Americans are asking: why do they hate us? They hate our freedoms—our freedom of religion, our freedom of speech, our freedom to vote and assemble and disagree with each other' (George W. Bush, in his speech in US Congress in the aftermath of 9/11 [2001]). The later history is mired with the gross abuse of international norms and violation of United Nations' political-moral authority. US went on to attack first Afghanistan and then Iraq. The 'brave front' put by US in a way turned to be counter productive in the long term. One of the results of the wars has been the worsening of economic scenario in US and also the world over.

II

With the 9/11 killing nearly 3,000 innocent people, US President George Bush went on to say that 'either you are with them (terrorists) or with us'. US media went on to popularize the word 'Islamic terrorism', which was picked up by the global media. Islam came to be presented as the religion standing for violence. Muslims world over started to be perceived as terrorists, as the formulation, 'All Muslims are not terrorists but all Terrorists are Muslims' gained currency. On one hand, Muslims were intimidated all over and on the other, the radical Islamist groups, trained by US machinations, intensified their activities, especially in South Asia. Section of the community threatened due to this demonization started receding into the shell of religiosity, and the hold of fundamentalist mullahs over the community increased at places.

The concept of security world over got perverted and air travel became an exercise in proving one's citizenship at all the places, time and over again. The security measures getting tightened and insecurity increasing went hand in hand, as the core issue remained unanswered. One knows that the primary indoctrination of terrorists is to be ready to die for the 'cause'. The primary causes of terrorism have remained unanswered. The War on terror is a euphemism, plain and simple. Wars are generally against a well defined enemy. Terror is a concept, totally amorphous in character, with no fixed group or organization behind it.

In a way US was clear that the message behind War on terror is to attack the countries which are Muslim! Afghanistan was attacked presumably to catch hold of Osama bin Laden and destroy the terror network. Iraq was attacked on the pretext of Weapons of Mass Destructions (WMD), the weapons which eluded all the searchers as they were just not there. It is for the first time in the modern history that the colonial goals, imperialist agenda of plunder was clothed in religious language, when US media deliberately used the word 'Islamic terrorism'. At the same time US seemed to be working on the theory of 'clash of civilizations' propounded by Samuel Huntington, according to which the backward Islamic civilization is out to attack the West, so in turn they should be set right by various means (Huntington, 1995).

Unfortunately and mainly as the politics around identity issues started getting stronger, the conservative, orthodox and radical elements of Islam staked their claim to be real Islam. The intimidated Muslim societies at places gave in to them out of identity crisis of insecure communities. Thus the picture that all terrorists are Muslims, Islam is a religion of violence came to become the part of 'social common sense'. The global media gleefully followed this negative lead given by the US media. In India this propagation was enhanced and assisted by the Right wing politics at home.

III

The type of insanity displayed by the Al Qaeda–Taliban was both amazing and disturbing. The acts which they perpetuated were the limit of insanity, totally against the human values. We witnessed the global hysteria by sections of Muslims around this time. Many a global campaigns in which sections of Muslims participated out of a fanatic zeal brought great disrepute to Islam and Muslims in general.

Meanwhile, in India, particularly from 2006 various acts of terror in front of mosques, *dargah*s started taking place (Gatade, 2007). Already Muslim community was feeling battered due to the communal violence during the preceding decades. Sachar Committee report tells us that Muslim community has been relegated to the margins of society. Their economic status has declined during last 60 years (Sachar Committee, 2004). On top of that, the acts of terror started becoming clearly targeted at Muslim community, like the Malegaon blast, Mecca Masjid blast in Hyderabad, Samjhauta Express and Ajmer Sharif Dargah. The investigating agencies were clueless. Usually many Muslim youth were caught, tortured to elicit confession and in most cases released after no evidence could be established. The community's insecurity went up further (Statement of the People's Tribunal, Hyderabad).

The pattern kept repeating itself. In Nanded, in 2006, two Bajrang Dal workers died while making bombs (Gatade, www.Countercurrents.org/gatade011007.html). In the same city, later, a Shiv Sena Shakha member died in the godown storing biscuits, two Bajrang Dal workers died in Kanpur in 2008, and many such incidents kept going on. The tide in a way turned when the irrefutable evidence of Sadhvi Pragya Singh Thakurs' motorcycle, used in the Malegaon blast was detected. The immaculate investigation done by Mahrashtra ATS led to the detection of the involvement of other RSS affiliates (meaning all those organizations who subscribe to RSS ideology of Hindu Nation, Hindutva and whose core team is trained by the volunteers of RSS *shakha*s), Swami Dayanand Pandey, Lt Col. Prasad Purohit, Retired Major Upadhyay and many others including Swami Assemanand of VHP in Dangs. Sadhvi's photo was also seen with the BJP President Rajnath Singh (Appendix I). This shocking revelation brought the truth of terror attacks from a different dimension. 'Hemant's (Karkare) team […] had arrested Hindu extremists in a breakthrough that shocked the entire nation and added a new dimension to the subject of terror and Hindutva politics in India. But the case got caught in political circus and ATS was accused of targeting the Hindu Nationalist Brigade' (Khetan, 2009).

So far the word 'Islamic terrorism' was being used with gay abandon. Now the term Hindu terrorism came to be coined spontaneously. Rightly, serious objection was raised against the use of this word. As Malegaon investigation showed, more and more involvement of those close to Hindutva ideology, the word Hindu terrorism propped up, 'The death of Hemant Karakre, the Chief of Maharashtra ATS in the battle against jehadi terrorists in Mumbai, puts the recent squabbles over the term "Hindu" terror in perspective. The alleged involvement of Sadhvi Pragya Singh Thakur […] with terrorist explosions in

Malegaon had lazy journalists using term as a kind of tabloid shorthand' (Kesvan, 2009). The RSS affiliates started hurling abuses on the Maharashtra ATS Chief Hemant Karkare, calling him Deshdrohi (traitor) for the investigation work which he was pursuing. *Saamna*, the Shiv Sena mouthpiece, wrote an editorial that they spit on a person like Hemant Karkare for doing the investigation (*Outlook*, 15 December 2008). What type of pressure it must have generated on the mind of Karkare can be easily guessed. Some of these aspects do get reflected in the chapters of this compilation. It became clear that the association of terrorism and Muslims may not hold much water and with reluctance some section of media and popular opinion started desisting from demonizing Muslims, which it has been doing so far.

The role of Maharashtra ATS and especially its Chief Karkare's forthright stand in honest investigation was coming in the way of Hindutva groups, merrily involved in acts of terror, acts which were being passed off as the one's done by Muslims.

IV

In India, Pakistan has been seen as a source of terrorism and time and again there have been loud noises calling for attack on Pakistan. In the wake of 26/11 act of terror, when the link of terrorists to Pakistan was clear, there was a hue and cry to attack Pakistan. The popular yoga guru Baba Ramdeo, reflecting the opinion of a section of population, went to the extent of exhorting the government to launch an attack on Pakistan, and that if the government had financial difficulties, he would fund the war! The global media was also agog with similar sentiment, 'If you go over the coverage of the attacks in British and American newspapers you will find that all the articles focused on the imminent India-Pakistan war and, then, on the almost certain Hindu backlash that would lead to targeting of local Muslims' (Sanghavi, 2009, p. IV). In the peace marches, the candle marches which showed the resolve of the major section of society for peace, some of the fanatic elements did enter in the marches which ultimately started shouting anti-Pakistan slogans. Indian government had a tough time but it did take a reasoned position. Indian government systematically confronted the Pakistan government but the understanding was, 'Pakistan's civilian Government is not complicit in the Mumbai attacks, it was engineered by rouge elements in ISI and the army. War could weaken Zardari Govt... Not in India's interest' (Sharma, 2009). One notes that after the 26/11 Mumbai attack, many and much worse attacks took place in Pakistan itself, 'The choice of targets in Mumbai clearly owes something to the September bombing of the Islamabad Marriot, Here already there is a common ground between the two countries—for if it has been a bad year for India, then for Pakistan it has been much worse' (Ghosh, 2009).

While it is true that many a terror groups are housed in Pakistan, all of them cannot be attributed to the Government of Pakistan which currently is a democratic set-up. Pakistan is a creation of tragic events that took place during the freedom movement.

Apart from other things, British policy of divide and rule has been a major factor in creation of Pakistan. The Pakistan, formed in the name of Islam, rapidly came to be dominated by fundamentalist elements, and their military and mullahs had pre-eminent position. Starting from Field Marshal Ayub Khan to the Musharraf regime, the military–mullah complex has been in the forefront of affairs most of the time. The interlude of rules of Benazir Bhutto, Nawaz Sharif and now Asif Ali Zardari regime are the exceptions to the overall political trend in Pakistan. And lately it seems that democracy may be there to stay in Pakistan.

With the Al Qaeda training camps persisting on the soil of Pakistan, the tragedy for Pakistan society was immense. The heartening thing has been the effort of democratic elements to come back and to strive to strengthen the nascent democratic roots there. The democratic government and civic society are strongly fighting against the menace of terrorism. The people of Pakistan are fed up of the acts of terror; they despise the dominance of mullahs and dread the army coming back to power. So within Pakistan there are different players. The compulsions of Pakistan Government and civil society need to be perceived empathetically. They themselves are the big victims of terrorist acts.

This is a challenging task. Bilateral talks, mutual cooperation in weeding out terrorist groups, in undermining the military–mullah dominance are what is needed. Now South Asians need to come together to deal with the problem of terrorism. An attack on

Pakistan will only strengthen the retrograde elements in Pakistan, the military in particular. There must be an open transparent policy towards Pakistan and by mutual cooperation with the civic society and the elected government we should try to overcome the problems which are afflicting South Asia.

V

As this compilation is an attempt to analyze the phenomenon, the focus in selection has been for articles that are more analytic than descriptive. Hidden in every event are the deeper issues related to the phenomenon. The contributors in the volume have tried to analyze the event from various angles, terrorism, law, Indo-Pak relations, the causes of terrorism in India, role of state, pattern of investigations so far, the prevalent laws, the response of civic society, the role of media, the unsolved puzzles and need for a deeper inquiry into the event. Most of the chapters have been written in the immediate aftermath of the tragedy and bear the imprint of pain and anguish caused by the event with mammoth tragedies hidden in the same.

Anand Patwardhan in his 'Terror: The Aftermath' questions the need for new, tough anti-terror laws, which was the cry of a section. This chapter laments the gradual shift of India's foreign policy from one of non-alignment to the one which is trying to be subservient to US and is tilting towards Israel. The safety of the country just cannot come by increasing the security. Also the double standards which have been pursued by India in the matters relating to justice to minorities after communal violence is sowing the seeds of dissatisfaction which may be the starting point for some turning to this insane path of terror. He points out that since Hemant Karkare was criticized heavily by the leaders of RSS combine, he might have been under pressure to prove himself leading to his throwing the caution to wind and becoming the victim of violence.

Guantanamo Bay had become synonymous with inhuman torture, with throwing the human rights and any human consideration to the wind to extract confessions in the wake of 9/11. This was also synonymous with how a state, and that too claiming to be the biggest democracy in the world, can fall to abysmal levels. Mercifully Barack Hussein Obama's initial orders were to close down this blot on the face of democratic governments. This is what has been disturbing Biju Mathew in his 'As the Fires Die: The Terror of the Aftermath'. Mathew points out that in the massive Guantanamo Bay there has not been even a single breakthrough. An example as to how states also can get insane if they pursue the policy out of anger rather than out of reason. The post 9/11 polices of US had been a disaster, the Patriot Act, the invasion on Afghanistan and Iraq. These polices have not only increased the grip of fundamentalist forces all over, they might have contributed to the economic downfall of the mighty empire.

Gnani Sankaran, in his 'Hotel Taj: Icon of Whose India?' takes up the issue of media projection that Taj is the icon of Mumbai/India. During this attack

Chatrapati Shivaji Terminus, popularly known as V.T., J.J. Hospital, Cama Hospital and Taj and Trident were the sites where many people died. Taj and Trident were presented as icons of Mumbai. These are the upmarket hotels, frequented by the five star people, celebrities and business tycoons. When previously the attacks took place on the trains and buses, the media projection was on resilience of the people in facing the terror acts. Now when the top brass is also involved the slogan was not resilience but 'enough is enough'. Should these places be called icons of Mumbai? Sankaran argues that they are not, as they do not represent average Mumbaikar.

How US committed the big blunder after 9/11 attack is brought out forcefully by P. Sainath in 'Why the United States Got it Wrong?' In the wake of the killing of 180 people in the terror attack the argument was that like US, India should attack Pakistan. See how due to US action in the wake of 9/11 in 2001, no further terror attacks took place in US. Sainath argues that the biggest beneficiary of US action has been Al Qaeda while Pakistan has been the biggest victim of US policies. The invasion on Iraq by US cost it 3 trillion dollars and the consequent impact on its economy. He also takes on media for preparing ground for US invasion through 'embedded stories' which created a popular sanction for the dastardly US action on the people of Iraq. In Iraq the mortality rate of 5.5 per thousand has jumped up to 13.3 per thousand after the invasion by US. Also from the invading US army over a hundred thousand cases of mental illness have been reported. So much for the bravado of US action!

One has to thank the people of India for ensuring that the Indian government did not and will not undertake such insane step.

'Death of a Salesman' by Tarun Tejpal takes up the rot which has set in the society. While we blame politician, we at the same time overlook the deeper rot which is becoming rooted in the society. Our tolerance for injustice, discrimination against weaker section of society, violence against minorities is creating a situation where we are failing as a system. We should look deeper and see that injustice breeds injustice and creates a situation where there is an all-round apathy. Mere blaming the politicians will not do, what is needed is a political overhaul of the system, and in this all will have to plunge, in case we want to make a success of it.

Praful Bidwai, in 'Counter-Terrorism Must not Kill Democracy', warns that the measures to counter terrorism should not kill democracy. According to him the fact that Antulay had asked a question, his question should not have been undermined. But unfortunately Antulay himself staged a climb down. UPA bringing in new laws is more of a caving in to the pressure of right wing than a necessity. The new laws are giving more power to the investigating agencies, at the cost of rights of the accused, and will not serve any purpose. Also The Prevention of Terrorism Act (POTA), the dreaded act, has been misused against the minorities. In another of his contribution to this volume, Bidwai argues that war is not the way and what is needed is diplomacy and restraint. This was in response to the immense hysterical atmosphere created by all-round, part of which was calling for war of different types, response to the 26/11 Mumbai attack.

Yoginder Sikand in his piece focuses more on the issues related to Islam, Lashkar-e-Taiba and armed jihad. He clarifies that Islam does not permit killing of the innocents on any grounds and that these aberrant groups like Lashkar are the offshoot of the same CIA–ISI–Madrassa trained fanatics, created for the political goals of the Empire. One point which has been missed out or rather not analyzed seriously is the report that the huge quantities of food was ordered from Nariman House ahead of the attack. And the very choosing of Nariman point, the possible role of Mossad in destabilizing the area should be kept in mind, while coming to conclusions about the issue.

Taking the issue of questions raised by Antulay, Ram Puniyani points out that the 1992–93 riots were followed by Mumbai blasts. The Maharashtra ATS Chief Karkare was called Deshdrohi, traitor, by RSS associates. He had also received death threat from anonymous sources. Antulay had made a simple point that the death of Karakre should be investigated, as he doubted that he might have been killed by terrorism plus something. It was good that the Maharashtra government has decided to probe this death, while Antulay who raised the question was called Pakistan supporter. At the same time, Shiv Sena went out of the way to provide legal aid for Malegaon blast-accused Sadhvi Pragya Singh Thakur. As such, in a democratic society, the matters should be transparent and raising queries should not be met with severe allegations from those in power or those right wingers who have been hurling abuses at the human rights activists raising questions and doubts about the state version of thing.

Raveena Hansa, in two of her chapters, pieces together all the versions of the incident presented by the media, and demonstrates the gaping holes in the different versions of the incident. Putting together all the news items which came out she shows that there may be something more serious behind the attack, than meets the eye. How can one version say that Karkare died near Metro, and another that he died in lane behind Cama Hospital? How can the terrorist speak fluent Marathi? Why was Kasab wearing the orange wrist band on his hand? Even the dossier submitted by the Indian government to Pakistan is not consistent in the narration of events. The point is why such an episode of severe order not be subjected to an honest probe? Who is against such a probe? She argues that even earlier many spectacular incidents were taken on the face value and those doubting them were labelled as one's believing in conspiracy theory. In case of John Kennedy's murder also doubts persist about the correctness of the state version of the tragedy. Similarly in the case of 9/11 attack on WTC, there is enough evidence to doubt the official version. In such cases the best option is to properly investigate the event, ignoring those making loud noises in the name of patriotism. Raveena Hansa is not alone in raising these uncomfortable questions; the point is, can the civic society and the state wake up and set the matters straight rather than abuse those raising these questions.

K.G. Balakrishnan, in 'Terrorism, Rule of Law and Human Rights', laments that there are no clear norms for international cooperation in cases where more than one country is involved. To accept the confessions before the police authorities goes against the norms of personal liberty. He does concede that the government need not necessarily be part of the conspiracy originating on its soil. There is a need to increase the acts of surveillance against acts of terror and also the need to introduce thorough professionalism in matters related to investigation of acts of terrorism.

Sukla Sen's 'Acts of Terror and Terrorizing Act' takes up the demand by some for introduction of draconian acts for prevention of terror acts. He points out that coercive interrogation generally leads to false confessions, which in turn may hide the truth from coming out. There is a failure of intelligence gathering due to the unfriendly image of the police, because of which there is a severance of police–people contact.

In 'Our Politicians are Still not Listening', Colin Gonsalves takes on the issue of criticizing the human rights activists rather than taking up proposals to combat terrorism. The new laws giving more detention time will not serve the purpose and are totally against the international legal norms. What is needed is to upgrade the CBI and bring in more professionalism to curb the acts of terror. Prashant

Bhushan, in 'Terrorism: Are Stronger Laws the Answer', is very critical of the present demands for more stringent laws. His contention is that no law can deter suicidal terrorists. POTA has been really an instrument to harass the minorities. People's tribunal on POTA pointed out that it is a law to terrorize ordinary citizens. Similarly the tribunal on terrorism also concluded that many an innocent Muslim youths have been targeted in the aftermath of acts of terror. He points out that there is an urgent need to implement the much overdue police reforms.

Piecing together different issues, Gautam Navlakha takes up the lapses in response to the terrorist attack. He questions the need for new laws in dealing with the acts of terror. He does point out that a look at deeper issues leading to acts of terror need to be kept in mind. There is great amount of 'Pakistan' and 'minority' obsession in investigating these cases. How the investigation into the acts of terror are coloured by religion is very clear as in most of the cases like Samjhauta Express blast, Mecca Masjid and Ajmer Sharif where the investigation was directed, misguided by religious identity till Sadhvi's motorcycle was found at the Malegaon blast case and the truth of most of the blasts started coming out. The total hostility to Pakistan in such matters is also misplaced as there are non-state actors. There is also a need to look at internal factors which have gone in to promote terrorism in the region.

VI

The current phenomenon of terrorism is multi-layered. The global politics for controlling oil wells, the unsolved ethno-national issues, the rise of communal violence and discrimination of minorities are all contributing to the process. So a simple solution of all this cannot be conceptualized. We need an honest investigation to come to conclusions about, 'who's done it'. What is needed is countering the popular notions of association of terrorism with a particular religion and religious community. Primary cause of this perception has been the formation of Madrassas in Pakistan, the formation of Al Qaeda to begin with.

Investigating acts of terror has been a very demanding challenge. This is the observation in many a post-blast cases, Mecca Masjid, Hyderabad, in particular. In this case many a Muslim youth were caught for the act. The same were released after six months when no evidence could be found. Same was the case in Jaipur blasts in which again many a Muslim youths were caught hold of. Such biased understanding did two damages. On one hand, it resulted in many innocent Muslim youths being caught and tortured. 'The people's Tribunal on Atrocities Committed against the minority in the name of fighting terrorism' under the leadership of Justice Sardar Ali Khan and Justice Bhargava (www.anhad.net/articles44.html) pointed out in its interim observations that 'the testimonies showed that a large number of young Muslims have been victimized by police on charge of being involved in various terrorist acts across the country'.

On the other hand, what will be the long-term social and psychological impact of such an attitude on the community as a whole and on the youth who have been subjected to humiliation and torture for no fault of theirs. Its repercussions cannot be undermined. When a wrong person is being implicated, at the same time the real culprit is getting away with his crime. This must be emboldening for that group to carry on with their dastardly crimes all over again after a period of time.

The chapters in this compilation make it abundantly clear that post 26/11 some things are being ignored and undermined. Let us for a moment think could there have been a possibility of thinking that those associated with RSS ideology can also be involved in such acts till Maharashtra ATS dug out the irrefutable evidence against Sadhvi Pragya Singh Thakur, Lt Col. Upadhaya and other associates of theirs? Even the Nanded blasts and other blasts where Bajrang Dal workers died while making bombs did not alert the investigating authorities to recognize that there can be other factors responsible than just Muslim youth. It also shows the severe communalization of social space. In such a scenario those raising queries and doubts should not be brushed aside or intimidated or labelled. The best answer to such queries is an impartial and professionally conducted investigation.

If we do say let truth prevail, then why so much anger and labelling against those demanding for truth to come out? Who benefits by hiding truth, and who is afraid of truth, is the question this compilation raises.

References

Baweja, Harinder. 2009. *26/11 Mumbai Attacked*, p. xi. New Delhi: Roli Books.

Gatade, Subhash. 2007. 'Saffron Terror', *Himal Magazine*, 20(10/11), October–November: 47–51. Available online at www.Countercurrents.org/gatade011007.html, accessed on 28 June 2008.

Ghosh, Amitav. 2009. 'Defeat or Victory isn't Determined by Success of Strike Itself, but by Response', in Vir Sanghavi (ed.), *The Attack on Mumbai*, pp. 82–84. New Delhi: Penguin.

Hensman, Rohini. 2002. *Terrorism, Imperialism and War*, p. 29. Mumbai: Build.

Huntington, Samuel. 1995. *The Clash of Civilizations and the Remaking of World Order*. New York: Simon and Schuster.

Kesvan, Mukul. 2009. 'ATS Chief was Doing his Job—Both in Malegaon and Mumbai', in *The Attack on Mumbai*, p. 71. Penguin.

Khetan, Chris. 2009. 'Bravehearts', in *26/11 Mubai Attacked*. Roli.

Koshy, Ninan. 2002. *War on Terror*. Delhi: Left Word.

Mamdani, Mahmood. 2005. *Good Muslim Bad Muslim*. Delhi: Permanent Black.

Mehta, Vinod. 2008. 'Ah Bombay', *Outlook*, 8 December.

Outlook. 2008. 'Heroes and Villains', *Outlook*, 15 December: 6.

People's Tribunal, Hyderabad, Anhad. www.anhad.net/articles44.html

Roy, Arundhati. 2002. *Algebra of Infinte Justice*. p. 127. Delhi: Penguin.

Sachar Committee. 2004. 'Social, Economic and Educational Status of the Muslim Community of India', November. Prime Ministers High Level Committee, Government of India.

Sanghavi, Vir. 2009. *26/11: The Attack on Mumbai*, p. viii. New Delhi: Penguin.

Sharma, Pranay. 2009. 'Soft Stricken', *Outlook*, 15 December: 30.

1

Terror: The Aftermath*

ANAND PATWARDHAN

The attack on Mumbai is over. After the numbing sorrow comes the blame game and the solutions. Loud voices amplified by saturation TV: Why do not we amend our Constitution to create new anti-terror laws? Why do not we arm our police with AK-47s? Why do not we do what Israel did after Munich or the USA did after 9/11 and hot pursue the enemy? Solutions that will lead us further into the abyss, for terror is a self-fulfilling prophecy! It thrives on reaction, polarization, militarization and the thirst for revenge.

The External Terror

Those who invoke America need only to analyze if its actions after 9/11 increased or decreased global terror. It invaded oil-rich Iraq fully knowing that Iraq had nothing to do with 9/11, killing over 200,000 Iraqi citizens but allowed a cornered Bin Laden to escape from Afghanistan. He recruited global support for Islamic militancy, which began to be seen as a just resistance against American mass murder, which begs the question of who created Bin Laden

*The article was earlier published in http://akivahb.wordpress.com/2008/12/10/terror-the-aftermath-by-anand-patwardhan

in the first place, armed the Madrassas of Pakistan and rejuvenated the concept of Islamic jihad? Israel played its own role in stoking the fires of jihad. The very creation of Israel in 1948 robbed Palestinians of their land, an act that Mahatma Gandhi to his credit deplored at that time as an unjust way to redress the wrongs done to Jews during the Holocaust. What followed has been a slow and continuing attack on the Palestinian nation. At first Palestinian resistance was led by secular forces represented by Yasser Arafat but as these were successfully undermined, Islamic forces took over the mantle. The first, largely non-violent Intifada was crushed, a second more violent one replaced it and when all else failed, human bombs appeared.

Thirty years ago when I first went abroad there were two countries my Indian passport forbade me to visit. One was racist South Africa. The other was Israel. We were non-aligned and stood for disarmament and world peace. Today Israel and America are our biggest military allies. Is it surprising that we are on the jihadi hit list? Israel, America and other prosperous countries can to an extent protect themselves against the determined jihadi, but can India put an impenetrable shield over itself? Remember that when attackers are on a suicide mission, the strongest shields have crumbled. New York was laid low not with nuclear weapons but with a pair of box cutters. India is for many reasons a quintessentially soft target. Our huge population, vast landmass and coastline are impossible to protect. The rich may build new barricades. The Taj and the

Oberoi can be made safer. So can our airports and planes. Can our railway stations and trains, bus stops, buses, markets and lanes do the same?

The Terror Within

The threat of terror in India does not come exclusively from outside. Apart from being hugely populated by the poor, India is also a country divided, not just between rich and poor, but by religion, caste and language. This internal divide is as potent a breeding ground for terror as jihadi camps abroad. Nor is jihad the copyright of one religion alone. It can be argued that, international causes apart, India has jihadis that are fully home grown. Perhaps the earliest famous one was Nathuram Godse who, acting at the behest of his mentor Vinayak Savarkar (still referred to as 'Veer' or 'brave' although he refused to own up to his role in the conspiracy), murdered Mahatma Gandhi for the crime of championing Muslims.

Jump forward to 6 December 1992, the day Hindu fanatics demolished the Babri Masjid setting into motion a chain of events that still wreaks havoc today. From the Bombay riots of 1992 to the bomb blasts of 1993, the Gujarat pogroms of 2002 and hundreds of smaller deadly events, the last 16 years have been the bloodiest since the Partition. Action has been followed by reaction in an endless cycle of escalating retribution. At the core on the Hindu side of terror are organizations that openly admire Adolph Hitler, nursing the hate of historic wrongs inflicted by Muslims. Ironically these votaries of Hitler remain friends and admirers of Israel.

On the Muslim side of terror are scores of disaffected youth, many of whom have seen their families tortured and killed in more recent pogroms. Christians too have fallen victim to recent Hindutva terror but as yet not formed the mechanisms for revenge. Dalits, despite centuries of caste oppression, have not yet retaliated in violence although a small fraction is being drawn into an armed struggle waged by Naxalites.

It is clear that no amount of spending on defence, no amount of patrolling the high seas, no amount of increasing the military and police and equipping them with the latest weaponry can end the cycle of violence or place India under a bubble of safety. Just as nuclear India did not lead to more safety, but only to a nuclear Pakistan, no amount of homeland security can save us. And inviting Israel's Mossad and America's CIA/FBI to the security table is like giving the anti-virus contract to those who spread the virus in the first place. It can only make us more of a target for the next determined jihadi attack.

Policing, Justice and the Media

As for draconian anti-terror laws, they too only breed terror as for the most part they are implemented by a state machinery that has imbibed majoritarian values. So in Modi's Gujarat after the ethnic cleansing of Muslims in 2002, despite scores of confessions to rape and murder captured on hidden camera, virtually no Hindu extremists were punished while thousands of Muslims rotted in jail under draconian laws. The same happened in Bombay despite the Shiv Sena being found guilty by the Justice Shrikrishna Commission.

Under pressure a few cases were finally brought to trial but all escaped with the lightest of knuckle raps. In stark contrast many Muslims accused in the 1993 bomb blasts were given death sentences.

The bulk of our media, police and judicial systems swallow the canard that Muslims are by nature violent. Removing democratic safeguards guaranteed by the Constitution can only make this worse. Every act of wrongful imprisonment and torture is likely to turn innocents into material for future terrorists to draw upon. Already the double standards are visible. While the Students Islamic Movement of India is banned, Hindutva outfits like the RSS, the VHP, the Bajrang Dal and the Shiv Sena remain legal entities. The leader of the MNS, Raj Thackeray, recently openly spread such hatred that several north Indians were killed by lynch mobs. Amongst these were the Dube brothers, doctors from Kalyan who treated the poor for a grand fee of Rs 10 per patient. Raj Thackeray, like his uncle Bal before him, remains free after issuing public threats that Bombay would burn if anyone had the guts to arrest him. Modi remains free despite the pogroms of Gujarat. Congress party murderers of Sikhs in 1984 remain free. Justice in India is clearly not there for all. Increasing the powers of the police cannot solve this problem. Only honest and unbiased implementation of laws that exist can.

It is a tragedy of the highest proportions that one such honest policeman, Anti-terrorist Squad Chief Hemant Karkare, who had begun to unravel the thread of Hindutva terror was himself gunned down, perhaps by Muslim terror. It is reported that

Col. Purohit and fellow Hindutva conspirators, now in judicial custody, celebrated the news of Karkare's death. Until Karkare took charge, the Malegaon bomb blasts in which Muslims were killed and the Samjhauta Express blasts in which Pakistani visitors to India were killed were being blamed on Muslims. Karkare exposed a hitherto unknown Hindutva outfit as masterminding a series of killer blasts across the country. For his pains Karkare came under vicious attack not just from militant Hindutva but from the mainstream BJP. He was under tremendous pressure to prove his patriotism. Was it this that led this senior officer to don helmet and ill-fitting bullet proof vest and rush into battle with a pistol? Or was it just his natural instinct, the same courage that had led him against all odds, to expose Hindutva terror?

Whatever it was, it only underlines the fact that jihadis of all kinds are actually allies of each other. So Bin Laden served George Bush and vice versa. So Islamic and Hindutva jihadis have served each other for years. Do they care who dies? Of the 200 people killed in the last few days by Islamic jihadis, a high number were Muslims. Many were waiting to board trains to celebrate Eid in their hometowns in Uttar Pradesh and Bihar, when their co-religionists gunned them down. Shockingly the media has not commented on this, nor focused on the tragedy at the railway station, choosing to concentrate on tragedies that befell the well-to-do. And it is the media that is leading the charge to turn us into a war-mongering police state where we may lead lives with an illusion of safety, but with the certainty of joylessness.

I am not arguing that we do not need efficient security at public places and at vulnerable sites. But real security will only come when it is accompanied by real justice, when the principles of democracy are implemented in every part of the country, when the legitimate grievances of people are not crushed, when the arms race is replaced by a race for decency and humanity, when our children grow up in an atmosphere where religious faith is put to the test of reason. Until such time we will remain at the mercy of 'patriots' and zealots.

2
As the Fires Die: The Terror of the Aftermath*

BIJU MATHEW

As the smoke lifts from Mumbai, skepticism must prevail over those conjectures which support the official state narrative. It is crucial to increase the pressure for transparency and accountability at this moment to ensure that India does not slide into the same state as post 9/11 USA.

The deaths continue even as I write this. The death toll stands at 195. And of the several hundred injured some may not survive. It is now official. The siege is over. The last of the gunmen inside the Taj Hotel has been shot dead. The other targets—the Leopold Cafe (a popular tourist hangout), the CST railway terminus (also called the Victoria Terminus), the Metro Cinema, the Cama Hospital—all seem to be targets the gunmen attacked as they zoned in on the hotels and Nariman House. In the end this has become a story of two sets of men with guns.

The human story of the innocents who died, the hotel staff who kept their cool and moved guests around the hotel through the service entryways and

---

*The article is already published in *Samar Marg* on 6 December 2008.

As the Fires Die | 9

exits, those who helped each other escape, will not really make it to the headlines. The maintenance worker at the Oberoi who shielded guests and took the bullets in his stomach will remain unsung. The hospital orderlies who ran in and out with stretchers carrying the wounded—each time not knowing if they will make it back themselves to the ambulance—will not be noted. The several trainee chefs at the Taj who fell to bullets even as other kitchen workers escorted guests away from the firing and hid them inside a private clubroom will not be written up in the book of heroes. The young waiter at Leopold who was to leave to work in a Cape Town restaurant will soon be forgotten. The two young men who dragged an Australian tourist shot in the leg away from the Leopold entrance and carried her to a taxi will not even identify themselves so that she can thank them. These stories, in as much as they are told, will remain on the lips of only the workers, the guests and the tourists who helped each other. The officials will try and produce a clean story to tell the world. And we know the clean story is untrue.

The official story that has already begun to emerge is one that may have some facts embedded in it. But we must remember that between every two facts is a lot of conjecture. The conjectures that unite the few facts (16 gunmen, AK-47s, grenades, passports of multiple nationalities, boats on which at least some of them arrived, a dead Anti-Terror Squad [ATS] chief, Hemant Karkare, who was heading the investigation against the Hindu Right wings' terror campaign, the gunmen trying to identify British and American citizens) makes the story. The story then is as much a product of the conjecture as it is of the facts. And there are certain stories that we are already oriented towards. The conjectures that create that story—the story we are already prepared for—is the one the state will dole out for our consumption. Already the conjectures that will serve the state are out there in great profusion.

Several reporters have noted that the gunmen were clean-shaven, dressed in jeans and T-shirts. The silent conjecture is that they were expecting and were surprised by the fact that these men did not have beards and did not sport the Muslim prayer cap. Every newspaper worth its salt—the *Times of India*, the *Jerusalem Post*, the *Independent* from the UK, among scores of others—has already run commentary on the unsecured coastline of India. The conjectural subtext is that securing the coastline is possible and if India had done so, this attack would have been prevented.

There is also a quick labelling going on—India's 9/11. The subtext is that India could and should act as the US did after 9/11—decisively and with great aggression. There is also the subtext that the Indian state is soft on terror that adds to the US tough-on-terror contrast. Sadanand Dhume, writing in the *Wall Street Journal*, has castigated the Indian government for withdrawing the Prevention of Terrorism Act (POTA) and for preventing states like Gujarat from passing their own version of the draconian worse-than-Patriot Act legislations. Neither Mr Dhume nor the several reporters, who will now write stories about how the POTA repeal represents the Indian state's soft attitude towards terror, will ever feel the need to explain how POTA could have prevented this attack.

The dead are on the floor. The vultures are moving in. The conjecture will try to unite the country into a series of unexamined positions. That POTA must be recalled. That states must be allowed to pass even more draconian laws. That Hindu terror is not a big issue and must be forgotten for now—especially now that we may not find an honest policeman or woman to head the ATS. That the defence budget must go up. That the coastline must be secured.

None of the well educated masters of the media will write that the 7,000 odd kilometre coastline cannot be protected—that all it will translate to is billions in contracts for all and sundry including Israeli and American consultants. Nobody will write that a hundred POTAs will not prevent a terror attack like this one; that Guantanamo Bay has not yielded a single breakthrough. Nobody will write that higher defence budgets have been more often correlated with insecure and militarized lives for ordinary citizens. Nobody will write that almost without exception all of US post 9/11 policies have been disasters. Bin Laden is still around, I am told, and so is the Al Qaeda. The number of fundamentalist Christians, Muslims, Hindus and Jews have probably gone up over the last decade. So much for good policy, but the conjecture will go on.

The foreign hand and its internal partner will be floated without ever naming anything precise. But the country will read it just as it is meant to be read—Pakistan and the Indian Muslim. Everything will rest on the supposed confession of the one gunman who has been captured. A Pakistani from Faridkot, I am told. Why should we believe it? Did not the same Indian state frame all the supposed accomplices in the Parliament attack case? Did not the same Indian state claim that the assassins of Chattisinghpura were from across the border until that story fell apart? And more recently, did not the same Indian state finally agree that all the accused in the Mecca Masjid bombings were actually innocent? And even if Mr Assassin supposedly from Faridkot did say what he did say—why should we believe him? Why is it so difficult to believe that he has his lines ready and scripted? If he was willing to die for whatever cause he murdered for, then can he not lie? Oh the lie detector test—that completely discredited science that every militarized state trots out. And the media love the lie detector test because it is the best scientific garb you can give to conjecture.

I certainly do not know the truth. But I do know that there is more than enough reason for skepticism. The problem is that we need a new theory of the state. We need to re-understand the state.

There is such unanimity when it comes to analyzing the Pakistani state—that the ISI, and if not all of the ISI, at least a segment of it, is a rogue element. Furthermore, that its bosses may not be sitting in Islamabad, but perhaps elsewhere in the country or even abroad. If we can accept that about the Pakistani state, why is it so difficult to accept it about the Indian state? We all know that Colin Powell was a kind of a patsy—a fall guy, who trotted out some lies on behalf of a segment of the neo-conservative movement firmly entrenched within the American state (which Obama will not touch). We also know that if the ISI has a rogue element in it, it was in good part created by the CIA. Then why do we think that the same guys could not render another state—such as the US—itself hollow from the inside.

The contemporary state is a different being. For every story of money-corruption you hear, there could just as well be one of political-corruption. Every vested interest who locates himself inside the state apparatus is not just a vested interest going after money but could just as well be securing the space for creating a certain politics. The RSS has a long history of trying to take over the bureaucracy, does it not? So do the neo-cons and so do the jamaatis. Then why do we believe in a theory of the state that is unified and with liberal goals?

The history of the liberal state and its relationship with capitalism of all types is a simple one. The longer that relationship persists the more corrupt and hollow the liberal state gets, leaving the space open for political ideologies to occupy its very insides. The logic for this is inherent in the very system. If profit is above all, then given the power the state has, it must be bought. Cheney is no different from Shivraj Patil, and Ambani is no different from Halliburton. They are both part of the story of hollowing the state out. And once the hollowing process begins, every ideological force can find its way in, as long as it has resources. The archetypal bourgeois liberal state is over. It never really existed, but what we have at the end of four decades of neo-liberalism bears no resemblance to the ideal formulation whatsoever. What we have instead is a series of hollowed out states with their nooks and crannies, their departments and offices populated with specific neo-conservative ideological interests. The US has its variant. India has its. And Israel its very own. It is incapable of delivering the truth, and not just the truth, it is only capable of producing lies.

If this story of skepticism makes sense then we have only one choice. To understand that it is crucial to increase the pressure for transparency at this moment, to be relentless in our demand for openness and detail, in our call to ensure that no investigation or inquiry that was in place be halted and that every one of these be subjected to public scrutiny. It is our responsibility to reject the discourse of secrecy based on security and demand specific standards of transparency. What we should demand is that every senior minister and every senior intelligence officer be examined and the records be made available to the public. What we must demand is that an officer of impeccable record be found to replace Hemant Karkare. What we must demand is that we get explanations of how a POTA clone would have stopped this crime. What we must ask is how POTA or the Patriot Act could have ever helped prevent terror? What we must do is support the Karkare family in their demand for a full investigation of his death in the company of the encounter specialist—Salaskar. What we must have is an open debate on every single case of terror over the last decade in India.

When I am in Bombay, I always stay at a friend's on Third Pasta Lane. Each afternoon I would walk out and see the Nariman House. I have wondered what the decrepit building was. I have always contrasted the drabness of the building with the colourful sign on the next building that announces Colaba Sweet House. The next time I would not wonder. I will know that it was one of the places where the drama that inaugurated India's renewed march towards fascism unfolded. Unless we act with speed and determination demanding transparency and accountability and a careful rewriting of the story of terror in India. Only a renewed movement can ensure that India does not slide into the same state as post 9/11 USA.

3
Hotel Taj: Icon of Whose India?*

GNANI SANKARAN

Watching at least four English news channels surfing from one another during the last 60 hours of terror strike made me feel a terror of another kind. The terror of assaulting one's mind and sensitivity with cameras, sound bites and non-stop blabbers. All these channels have been trying to manufacture my consent for a big lie called—Hotel Taj, the icon of India. Whose India, whose Icon?

It is a matter of great shame that these channels simply did not bother about the other icon that faced the first attack from terrorists—the Chatrapathi Shivaji Terminus (CST) railway station. CST is the true icon of Mumbai. It is through this railway station hundreds of Indians from Uttar Pradesh, Bihar, Rajasthan, West Bengal and Tamil Nadu have poured into Mumbai over the years, transforming themselves into Mumbaikars and built the Mumbai of today along with the Marathis and Kolis.

But the channels would not recognize this. Nor would they recognize the 30 odd dead bodies strewn all over the platform of CST. No Barkha Dutt went

*The article is already published in Openspace.org.in on 4 December 2008.

there to tell us who they were. But she was at Taj to show us the damaged furniture and reception lobby braving the guards. And the TV cameras did not go to the government-run J.J. hospital to find out who those 26 unidentified bodies were. Instead they were again invading the battered Taj to try in vain for a scoop shot of the dead bodies of the page 3 celebrities.

In all probability, the unidentified bodies could be those of workers from Bihar and Uttar Pradesh migrating to Mumbai, arriving by train at CST without cell phones and pan cards to identify them. Even after 60 hours after the CST massacre, no channel has bothered to cover in detail what transpired there.

The channels conveniently failed to acknowledge that the *aam aadmi*s of India surviving in Mumbai were not affected by Taj, Oberoi and Trident closing down for a couple of weeks or months. What mattered to them was the stoppage of BEST buses and suburban trains even for one hour. But the channels were not covering that aspect of the terror attack. Such information at best merited a scroll line, while the cameras have to be dedicated for real time thriller unfolding at Taj or Nariman Bhavan.

The so called justification for the hype the channels built around heritage site Taj falling down (CST is also a heritage site), is that Hotel Taj is where the rich and the powerful of India and the globe congregate. It is a symbol or icon of power of money and politics, not India. It is the icon of the financiers and swindlers of India. The Mumbai and India were built by the *aam aadmi*s who passed through CST and Taj was the oasis of peace and privacy for those who wielded power over these mass of labouring classes. Leopold club and Taj were the haunts of rich spoilt kids who would drive their vehicles over sleeping *aam aadmi*s on the pavement, the Mafiosi of Mumbai forever financing the glitterati of Bollywood (and also the terrorists), political brokers and industrialists.

It is precisely because Taj is the icon of power and not people, that the terrorists chose to strike.

The terrorists have understood after several efforts that the *aam aadmi* will never break down even if you bomb her markets and trains. He/she was resilient because that is the only way he/she can even survive.

Resilience was another word that annoyed the pundits of news channels and their patrons this time. What resilience, enough is enough, said Pranoy Roy's channel on the left side of the channel spectrum. Same sentiments were echoed by Arnab Goswami representing the right wing of the broadcast media whose time is now. Can Rajdeep be far behind in this game of one upmanship over TRPs? They all attacked resilience this time. They wanted firm action from the government in tackling terror.

The same channels celebrated resilience when bombs went off in trains and markets killing and maiming the *aam aadmi*s. The resilience of the ordinary worker suited the rich business class of Mumbai since work or manufacture or film shooting did not stop. When it came to them, the rich shamelessly exhibited their lack of nerves and refused to be resilient themselves. They cry for government intervention now to protect their private spas and swimming pools and bars and restaurants, similar to the way in which Citibank, General Motors and the ilk cry for government money when their coffers are emptied by their own ideologies.

The terrorists have learnt that the ordinary Indian is unperturbed by terror. For one whose daily existence itself is a terror of government sponsored inflation and market sponsored exclusion, pain is something he has learnt to live with. The rich of Mumbai and India Inc are facing the pain for the first time and learning about it just as the middle classes of India learnt about violation of human rights only during emergency, a cool 28 years after independence. And human rights were another favourite issue for the channels to whip at times of terrorism. Arnab Goswami in an animated voice wondered where were those champions of human rights now, not to be seen applauding the brave and selfless police officers who gave up their life in fighting terrorism. Well, the counter question would be where were you when such officers were violating the human rights of *aam aadmi*s. Has there ever been any 24 hour non-stop coverage of violence against dalits and adivasis of this country?

This definitely was not the time to manufacture consent for the extra legal and third degree methods of interrogation of police and army but Arnabs do not miss a single opportunity to serve their class masters, this time the jingoistic patriotism came in handy to whitewash the entire uniformed services.

The sacrifice of the commandos or the police officers who went down dying at the hands of ruthless terrorists is no doubt heart rending but in vain in a situation which needed not just bran but also brain.

Israel has a point when it says the operations were misplanned resulting in the death of its nationals here.

Karkares and Salaskars would not be dead if they did not commit the mistake of travelling by the same vehicle. It is a basic lesson in management that the top brass should never travel together in crisis. The terrorists, if only they had watched the channels, would have laughed their hearts out when the Chief of the Marine commandos, an elite force, masking his face so unprofessionally in a see through cloth, told the media that the commandos had no idea about the structure of the Hotel Taj which they were trying to liberate. But the terrorists knew the place thoroughly, he acknowledged.

Is it so difficult to obtain a ground plan of Hotel Taj and discuss operation strategy thoroughly for at least one hour before entering? This is something even an event manager would first ask for, if he had to fix 25 audio systems and 50 CCTVs for a cultural event in a hotel. Would not Ratan Tata have provided a plan of his ancestral hotel to the commandos within one hour considering the mighty apparatus at his and government's disposal? Are satellite pictures only available for terrorists and not the government agencies? In an operation known to consume time, one more hour for preparation would have only improved the efficiency of execution. Sacrifices become doubly tragic in unprofessional circumstances. But the *aam aadmi*s always believe that terror-shooters do better planning than terrorists. And the gullible media in a jingoistic mood would not raise any question about any of these issues.

They after all have their favourite whipping boy—the politician, the eternal entertainer for the non-voting rich classes of India.

Arnabs and Rajdeeps would wax eloquent on Manmohan Singh and Advani visiting Mumbai separately and not together showing solidarity even at this hour of national crisis. What a farce? Why can not these channels pool together all their camera crew and reporters at this time of national calamity and share the sound and visual bytes which could mean a wider and deeper coverage of events with such a huge human resource to command? Why should Arnab and Rajdeep and Barkha keep harping every five minutes that this piece of information was exclusive to their channel, at the time of such a national crisis? Is this the time to promote the channel? If that is valid, the politician promoting his own political constituency is equally valid. And the duty of the politician is to do politics, his politics. It is for the people to evaluate that politics. And terrorism is not above politics. It is politics by other means.

To come to grips with it and to eventually eliminate it, the practice of politics by proper means needs constant fine tuning and improvement. Decrying all politics and politicians, only helps terrorists and dictators who are the two sides of the same coin. And the rich and powerful always prefer terrorists and dictators to do business with.

Those caught in this crossfire are always the *aam aadmi*s whose deaths are not even mourned—the taxi driver who lost the entire family at CST firing, the numerous waiters and stewards who lost their lives working in Taj for a monthly salary that would be one time bill for their masters.

Postscript: In a fit of anger and depression, I sent a message to all the channels, 30 hours through the coverage. After all they have been constantly asking the viewers to message them for anything and everything. My message read: I send this with lots of pain. All channels, including yours, must apologize for not covering the victims of CST massacre, the real Mumbaikars and *aam aadmi*s of India. Your obsession with five star elite is disgusting. Learn from the print media please. No channel bothered. Only Srinivasan Jain replied: you are right. We are trying to redress balance today. Well, nothing happened till the time of writing this 66 hours after the terror attack.

4
Why the United States Got it Wrong*

P. SAINATH

Of all the arguments making the rounds after the appalling slaughter of 180 people in Mumbai, the worst is this: that India should learn from the United States about how to respond to such terror. 'Look at the USA', goes the refrain, 'after 9/11 has there been another attack on U.S. soil?' In short, Washington's measures after that tragedy were so effective, nobody ever bothered them again. This knocks at the doors of insanity. The US 'response' does stand out as worth learning from. There is very little it did not get wrong.

Around 3,000 people lost their lives in the dreadful attacks on the World Trade Centre in New York on 9/11. America's response was to go to war. It launched two wars, one against a country that had not a single link to the events of 9/11. Close to a million human beings have lost their lives in that response. That includes 4,000 US troops in Iraq and nearly 1,000 in Afghanistan. That is apart from several hundred thousand Iraqis losing their lives. Countless Afghans die each month, as one of the world's poorest

*The article has already been published in *The Hindu*, 11 December 2008.

states sinks deeper into devastation. (Afghanistan, for US liberals, is 'the good war'.) Millions have suffered dislocation and deprivation in the region.

$3 Trillion War

Nobel Laureate Joseph Stiglitz estimates that the Iraq war is costing the United States $3 trillion in all (about three times India's GDP). Good news for American corporations that make a killing every time there is large-scale killing, but not of much use to ordinary Americans. With the US economy in awful crisis, those costs are haemorrhaging. The war in Iraq was launched with 'intelligence' findings on 'weapons of mass destruction' (WMDs) being stockpiled in that country. And on the ground that Baghdad was linked to 9/11. This was the excuse for the 'response'. Both claims proved false. At the time, the US media played a huge role—its response— in planting fabricated WMD stories. That helped launch perhaps the most destructive conflict of our time. American costs also include tens of thousands wounded, injured and ill soldiers. With over 100,000 US soldiers 'returning from the war suffering serious mental health disorders, a significant fraction of which will be chronic afflictions' (Stiglitz and Bilmes, 2008). Besides, the war meant huge spending cuts at home. At the time of writing, California, the largest of American states, is mulling massive cuts. 'Its budget deficit is around $11 billion', says journalist and analyst Conn Hallinan. 'Just about a month's worth of war costs in Iraq and Afghanistan.'

By late 2006, a little over three years after that 'response' began, over 650,000 Iraqis were estimated to have lost their lives. A survey by researchers at the Johns Hopkins Bloomberg School of Public Health in Baltimore, Maryland and the Al Mustansiriya University in Baghdad put it bluntly: 'As many as 654,965 more Iraqis may have died since hostilities began in Iraq in March 2003 than would have been expected under pre-war conditions. The deaths from all causes—violent and non-violent—are over and above the estimated 143,000 deaths per year that occurred from all causes prior to the March 2003 invasion.' Iraq's overall mortality rate more than doubled from 5.5 deaths per 1,000 persons before the war began to 13.3 per 1,000 persons by late 2006.

Many more civilians have died since then, an extension of the USA's 'response' to 9/11. Pre-war Iraq was the Arab country most ruthless towards Islamic fundamentalists. Today, the latter wield enormous power in a country they had no base in. Fundamentalism harvested new recruiting fields—fertilized by US violence. It's worth learning this: Al Qaeda was the biggest beneficiary of the 'response' of the United States to 9/11 alongside US corporations. America's 'War on Terror'—produced far more terrorism in the world than there had been prior to that response.

There are other lessons in the US debacle. Almost every week now, the US bombs some part of Pakistan— its firm ally of decades. Civilians are routinely killed by this, and if Mr Obama's campaign promises are to be kept, this will go up. So will the appeal of fundamentalism amongst the affected.

This is Islamabad's reward for decades of faithful support to American military adventures in

Afghanistan. A lot of Pakistan's distress arises from the very kind of strategic ties with the United States that India's elite would so love to have themselves. Also, the resultant undermining of Pakistan is bad news for India. More fundamentalisms, more militancy, and worse, on both sides of the border.

'Embedded Journalism'

The media too have much to learn from the response of their US counterparts. The 'embedded journalism' that disgraced some of America's leading media institutions. Regardless of a bleating anti-war editorial, the *New York Times* will never live down its WMD stories. The very media that now mock George Bush propped him up at the time. Now they report how unpopular the war is, how silly he was. But the 'war for ratings' had already done damage hard to undo. It's both pathetic and funny: the very forces in the United States that saw only external and foreign reasons for all that had happened now advise India exactly the opposite—not to rush to any such conclusions. 'In coming days', says the *New York Times* for example, 'India will have to look inward to see where and how its government failed to protect its citizens.'

The damage of whipped up hysteria as part of the 'response' occurred within the United States, too. Sikhs in America became the targets of vicious hate crimes across the country after 9/11. Why? The demonizing for years of anyone with turbans and beards made them targets of 'retaliation'. One Sikh body says it has logged over 300 hate crimes against

Sikhs after 9/11. These include torching of a home, vandalizing of gurdwaras, vicious assaults and one death by shooting. This is the model to emulate?

Curbing of Civil Liberties

Globally, the barbaric prison camp at Guantanamo, from where several prisoners have been released as innocent after years of brutal torture, has been a widely criticized part of the American 'response'. Inside the United States, the curbing of civil liberties—a vital 9/11 response—was at its worst since the McCarthy period. The Patriot Act was just one symbol of these. And Mr Bush now ranks among the most despised US Presidents of all time. (Though he did succeed, in another constituency, in bringing more popularity to Osama bin Laden than Al Qaeda's leader could have dreamed of.)

There is a need for a strong and vigorous response to the appalling outrage in Mumbai. Parts of what that should be are obvious: bringing the guilty to book, revamping the intelligence networks, overhauling a range of security agencies, being more prepared. It is no less vital, though, that the immediate response also be to deny the authors of the outrage the success of their goal. To ensure that further polarization within Mumbai society along religious, sectarian lines does not occur. To make sure that innocent people are not killed or terrorized in the 'response'. To dump the notion that shredding civil liberties and democratic rights help anybody in any way. Shred chauvinism and jingoism, not the Constitution of India. To strongly counter those attempting to foment communal strife, regardless of which religion they belong to. To see there is no repeat of 1992–93 when close to a quarter of a million people fled the city in terror. That would be a great reply. But to learn from Mumbai's events that we should emulate America's response—at the very time when Americans are figuring out how poorly they were served by it—would be to repeat history both as tragedy and as farce.

References

New York Times. 2008. 'The Horror in Mumbai', *New York Times*, 30 November. Available online at http://www.nytimes.com/2008/1210/opinion/01mon1.html

Stiglitz, Joseph and Linda Bilmes. 2008. *The Three Trillion Dollar War*. London: Penguin (Allen Lame).

5
Death of a Salesman*

TARUN TEJPAL

Rohinton Maloo was shot doing two things he enjoyed immensely. Eating good food and tossing new ideas. He was among the 13 diners at the Kandahar, Trident-Oberoi, who were marched out onto the service staircase, ostensibly as hostages. But the killers had nothing to bargain for. The answers to the big questions—Babri Masjid, Gujarat, Muslim persecution—were beyond the power of anyone to deliver neatly to the hotel lobby. The small ones—of money and materialism—their crazed indoctrination had already taken them well beyond. With the final banality of all fanaticism, flaunting the paradox of modern technology and medieval fervour—AK-47 in one hand; mobile phone in the other—the killers asked their minders, '*Udan dein?*'(should we blow them up?). The minder, probably a maintainer of cold statistics, said, '*Uda do*' (blow them up).

Rohinton caught seven bullets, and by the time his body was recovered, it could only be identified by the ring on his finger. Rohinton was just 48,

---

*The article has already been published in *Tehelka* magazine, vol. 5, issue 49 on 13 December 2008.

with two teenage children, and a hundred plans. A few of these had to do with *Tehelka*, where he was a strategic advisor for the last two years. As Indians, we seldom have a good word to say about the living, but in the dead we discover virtues that strain the imagination. Perhaps it has to do with a strange mix of driving envy and blinding piety. Let me just say Rohinton was charismatic, ambitious and a man of his time, and place. The time was always now, and in his outstanding career in media marketing, he was ever at the cutting edge of the new—in the creation of Star Networks, and a score of ventures on the web. The place was always Mumbai, the city he grew up in and lived in, and he exemplified its attitudes: the hedonism, the get-go, the easy pluralism.

For me there is a deep irony in his death. He was killed by what he set very little store by. In his every meeting with us, he was bemused and baffled by *Tehelka*'s obsessive engagement with politics. He was quite sure no one of his class—our class—was interested in the subject. Politics happened elsewhere, a regrettable business carried out by unsavoury characters. Mostly, it had nothing to do with our lives. Eventually, sitting through our political ranting, he came to grudgingly accept we may have some kind of a case. But he remained unconvinced of its commercial viability. Our kind of readers were interested in other things, which were germane to their lives—food, films, cricket, fashion, gizmos, television, health and the strategies of seduction. Politics, at best, was something they endured.

In the end, politics killed Rohinton, and a few hundred other innocents. In the final count, politics, every single day, is killing, impoverishing, starving, denigrating, millions of Indians all across the country. If the backdrop were not so heartbreaking, the spectacle of the nation's elite—the keepers of most of our wealth and privilege—frothing on television screens and screaming through mobile phones would be amusing. They have been outraged because the enduring tragedy of India has suddenly arrived in their marbled precincts. The Taj, the Oberoi. We dine here. We sleep here. Is nothing sacrosanct in this country any more?

What the Indian elite is discovering today on the debris of fancy eateries is an acidic truth large numbers of ordinary Indians are forced to swallow every day. Children who die of malnutrition, farmers who commit suicide, dalits who are raped and massacred, tribals who are turfed out of century-old habitats, peasants whose lands are taken over for car factories, minorities who are bludgeoned into paranoia—these, and many others, know that something is grossly wrong. The system does not work, the system is cruel, the system is unjust, the system exists to only serve those who run it. Crucially, what we, the elite, need to understand is that most of us are complicit in the system. In fact, chances are the more we have—of privilege and money—the more invested we are in the shoring up of an unfair state.

It is time each one of us understood that at the heart of every society is its politics. If the politics is third-rate, the condition of the society will be no better. For too many decades now, the elite of India has washed its hands off the country's politics. Entire generations have grown up viewing it as a distasteful activity. In an astonishing perversion, the finest imaginative act of the last thousand years on the subcontinent, the creation and flowering of the idea of modern India through mass politics, has for the last 40 years been rendered infra dig, déclassé, uncool. Let us blame our parents, and let our children blame us, for not bequeathing onwards the sheer beauty of a collective vision, collective will, and collective action. In a word, politics: which, at its best, created the wonder of a liberal and democratic idea, and at its worst threatens to tear it down.

We stand faulted then in two ways. For turning our back on the collective endeavour; and for our passive embrace of the status quo. This is in equal parts due to selfish instinct and to shallow thinking. Since shining India is basically only about us getting an even greater share of the pie, we have been happy to buy its half-truths, and look away from the rest of the sordid story. Like all elites, historically, that have presided over the decline of their societies, we focus too much of our energy on acquiring and consuming, and too little on thinking and decoding. Egged on by a helium media, we exhaust ourselves through paroxysms over vacant celebrities and trivia, quite happy not to see what might cause us discomfort.

For years, it has been evident that we are a society being systematically hollowed out by inequality, corruption, bigotry and lack of justice. The planks of public discourse have increasingly been divisive, widening the faultlines of caste, language, religion, class, community and region. As the elite of the most complex society in the world, we have failed to see that we are ratcheted into an intricate framework, full of causal links, where one wrong word begets another, one horrific event leads to another. Where one man's misery will eventually trigger another's.

Let's track one causal chain. The Congress creates Jarnail Singh Bhindranwale to neutralize the Akalis; Bhindranwale creates terrorism; Indira Gandhi moves against terrorism; terrorism assassinates Indira Gandhi; blameless Sikhs are slaughtered in Delhi; in the course of a decade, numberless innocents, militants, and securitymen die. Let's track another. The BJP takes out an inflammatory *rath yatra*; inflamed *kar sewak*s pull down the Babri Masjid; riots ensue; vengeful Muslims trigger Mumbai blasts; 10 years later a bogey of *kar sewak*s is burnt in Gujarat; in the next week 2,000 Muslims are slaughtered; six years later retaliatory violence continues. Let's track one more. In the early 1940s, in the midst of the freedom movement, patrician Muslims demand a separate homeland; Mahatma Gandhi opposes it; the British support it; Partition ensues; a million people are slaughtered; four wars follow; two countries drain each other through rhetoric and poison; nuclear arsenals are built; hotels in Mumbai are attacked.

In each of these rough causal chains, there is one thing in common. Their origin in the decisions of the elite. Interlaced with numberless lines of potential divisiveness, the India framework is highly delicate and complicated. It is critical for the elite to understand the framework, and its role in it. The elite has its hands on the levers of capital, influence and privilege. It can fix the framework. It has much to give, and it must give generously. The mass, with nothing in its hands, nothing to give, can out of frustration and anger, only pull it all down. And when the volcano blows, rich and poor burn alike.

And so what should we be doing? Well, screaming at politicians is certainly not political engagement. And airy socialites demanding the carpet-bombing of Pakistan and the boycott of taxes are plain absurd, just another neon sign advertising shallow thought. It's the kind of dumb public theatre the media ought to deftly side-step rather than showcase. The world is already over-shrill with animus: we need to tone it down, not add to it. Pakistan is itself badly damaged by the flawed politics at its heart. It needs help, not bombing. Just remember, when hardboiled bureaucrats clench their teeth, little children die.

Most of the shouting of the last few days is little more than personal catharsis through public venting. The fact is that the politician has been doing what we have been doing, and as an über Indian he has been doing it much better. Watching out for himself, cornering maximum resource, and turning away from the challenge of the greater good.

The first thing we need to do is to square up to the truth. Acknowledge the fact that we have made a fair shambles of the project of nation-building. Fifty million Indians doing well does not for a great India make, given that 500 million are grovelling to survive. Sixty years after independence, it can safely be said that India's political leadership—and the nation's elite—have badly let down the country's dispossessed and wretched. If you care to look, India today is heartbreak hotel, where infants die like flies, and equal opportunity is a cruel mirage.

Let's be clear we are not in a crisis because the Taj hotel was gutted. We are in a crisis because six years after 2,000 Muslims were slaughtered in Gujarat there is still no sign of justice. This is the second thing the elite need to understand—after the obscenity of gross inequality. The plinth of every society—since the beginning of Man—has been set on the notion of justice. You cannot light candles for just those of your class and creed. You have to strike a blow for every wronged citizen.

And let no one tell us we need more laws. We need men to implement those that we have. Today all our institutions and processes are failing us. We have compromised each of them on their values, their robustness, their vision and their sense of fairplay. Now, at every crucial juncture we depend on random acts of individual excellence and courage to save the day. Great systems, triumphant societies, are veined with ladders of inspiration. Electrified by those above them, men strive to do their very best. Look around. How many constables, head constables, sub-inspectors would risk their lives for the dishonest, weak men they serve, who in turn serve even more compromised masters? The lottery of death in Mumbai last week. In an instant, he would have understood what we always went on about. India's crying need is not economic tinkering or social engineering. It is a political overhaul, a political cleansing. As it once did to create a free nation, India's elite should start getting its hands dirty so they can get a clean country.

6

Counter-terrorism Must not Kill Democracy*

PRAFUL BIDWAI

In a season in which politicians have become everybody's punching bag and targets of vicious media attacks, it would have been a miracle had Minister for Minority Affairs Abdul Rehman Antulay not attracted ridicule for demanding an inquiry into the killing of Maharashtra Anti-Terrorism Squad Chief Hemant Karkare and his colleagues Ashok Kamte and Vijay Salaskar. I am no admirer of Antulay. I was among the handful of journalists who exposed his brutal evacuation and expulsion of pavement-dwellers in Mumbai in 1983. Yet, the questions he posed about Karkare's death would not go away—despite his own ignominious climbdown.

Antulay did not allege that Karkare, who famously cracked the Hindutva terror network involving Pragya Thakur and Lt Col. Shreekant Purohit, was shot by one of its members. His query was, who asked Karkare to go to Mumbai's CST station and to Cama Hospital, near which he was killed by Abu Ismail and Ajmal Amir Kasab?

*The article is already published in countercurrents.org on 28 December 2008.

We still do not know what motivated Karkare's team to go there without high-grade bullet-proof jackets and in violation of the norm that senior officers should not travel in the same vehicle in an emergency. Home Minister P. Chidambaram's statement to Parliament does not clarify the issue. According to one police account aired on television, the team went to Cama Hospital to rescue another officer, Sadanand Date, who was injured. According to a second account, the team was pursuing a red car carrying Ismail and Kasab.

It is hard to believe that senior officers like Karkare, Kamte and Salaskar all had to walk to CST/Cama because the police had erected barricades, and that they abandoned their separate vehicles to get into one car while chasing the fugitives. Even the circumstances of Karkare's killing, allegedly in a narrow lane behind the hospital, remain obscure.

If the police wireless message about the red car was meant to lure the team into an ambush, it is vital to ask where and how the report originated. If the gunmen were firing from the left, as Constable Arun Jadhav—who was in Karkare's car, but survived the attack—said, how was Karkare hit three times in the chest while Jadhav got two bullets in his right arm? Also, the ambush story does not quite hang together. The only vegetation in the lane has wire netting around it, behind which it would be hard to hide.

Clearly, even if one discounts all conspiracy theories, unanswered questions remain. Hindutva groups reviled Karkare for his bold, scrupulous investigation into the Thakur–Purohit terror network. L.K. Advani, no less, wanted him removed from the Anti-Terrorist Squad (ATS) and levelled charges, disproved after medical examination, that Thakur was tortured in ATS custody. This, and the gaps in the police account(s), makes imperative a dispassionate, thorough, high-level investigation into his killing—in addition to an inquiry into the intelligence failures and state agencies' inept response to the attacks.

The case for an inquiry in the Karkare case is all the stronger because many in the Muslim community—which has borne the brunt of excesses committed in the name of fighting terrorism—and other citizens too, have seriously questioned the official account.

Antulay or no Antulay, it is the government's duty to answer them. Supremely callous colonial rulers ignore public concerns. But democratic governments' legitimacy depends on respecting them and sharing the truth with the public in the interests of social cohesion. A credible inquiry would help rebuild the public's faith in the government, which has recently suffered erosion.

There are moments in the life of a nation when exemplary rectitude, transparency and adherence to law are called for, and an effort worthy of universal respect is necessary to reach out to those who feel excluded. Justice H.R. Khanna's dissenting opinion in the Emergency case, Justice B.N. Srikrishna's inquiry into the Mumbai violence of 1992–93, and Karkare's own brilliant investigation into the Hindutva terror network, are instances of these. In each case, state functionaries rose above pressures to harness their work to extraneous agendas. The entire nation gained from their work. We badly need another such effort today.

Regrettably, the United Progressive Alliance government seems to be caving in to right-wing pressures from the Bharatiya Janata Party to adopt a macho, national-chauvinist, 'to-hell-with-civil-liberties' stance to show that it has the will to fight terrorism. That alone explains the deplorable haste with which it railroaded through Parliament two tough counter-terrorism laws without serious debate. These erode federalism and infringe civil liberties.

The National Investigation Agency Act establishes a new organization to investigate acts of terrorism and offences related to atomic energy, aviation, maritime transport, sedition, weapons of mass destruction and left-wing extremism. Significantly, it excludes Hindutva-style right-wing extremism, which has taken a far higher toll in India than left-wing Naxalism. It's far from clear how the NIA can secure the cooperation of other existing agencies, rather than face turf battles and sabotage.

Unlike the Central Bureau of Investigation, which needs the consent of a state before investigating crimes there, the NIA will supersede state agencies. This is a serious intrusion into the federal system. The NIA, and the special courts set up under the Act, will be vulnerable to political abuse by the centre.

The second law, the Unlawful Activities (Prevention) Amendment Act brings back the discredited The Prevention of Terrorism Act (POTA), except for admitting confessions made to the police as evidence. It radically changes criminal procedures, extends periods of police custody and detention without charges, denies bail to foreigners, and reverses the burden of proof in many instances. The Act will turn India into a virtual police state.

The UPA abrogated POTA in 2004 in response to innumerable complaints of abuse against Muslims and application to offences not connected with terrorism. But the UPA retained all other tough laws, and also amended the Unlawful Activities Act. This increased punishment for terrorism and harbouring/financing terrorists made communications intercepts admissible as evidence, and increased detention without charges to 90 days from 30 days.

However, despite numerous recent terrorist attacks, the UPA firmly rejected the BJP's demand that POTA be re-enacted. But now, it has shamefully caved in to the demand—under the pressure of elite opinion and with an eye on the next general election.

The Unlawful Activities (Prevention) Act (UAPA) contains a range of draconian clauses, including a redefinition of terrorism, harsh punishment like life sentence or death, long periods of detention and presumption of guilt in many cases. The redefinition includes acts done with the intent to threaten or 'likely' to threaten India's unity, integrity or sovereignty. Under this hold-all provision, the police can arrest, search and seize the property of anyone whom it 'has reason to believe from personal knowledge, or any information by any person... or any articles or any other thing...' Even rumours and baseless suspicion fit this description. Also covered are attempts to kidnap constitutional and other functionaries listed by the government. The list is endless.

Counter-terrorism Must not Kill Democracy | 41

Under the Act, an accused can be held in police custody for 30 days, and detained without charges for 180 days. This is a travesty of constitutional rights. Even worse is the presumption of guilt in case there is a recovery of arms, explosives and 'substances of a similar nature'. The police routinely plants arms and explosives, and creates a false recovery record. The punishment range extends from three or five years to life. This shows the government has not applied its mind.

Under the Act, there is a general obligation to disclose 'all information' that a police officer thinks might be relevant. Failure to disclose can lead to imprisonment for three years. Journalists, lawyers, doctors and friends are not exempt from this sweeping provision, which presumes guilt on mere suspicion. Besides making telecommunications and e-mail intercepts admissible as evidence, the Act also denies bail to all foreign nationals and to all others if a prima facie case exists on the basis of a First Information Report by the police.

POTA and its predecessor, the Terrorist and Disruptive Activities (Prevention) Act were extensively abused. They targeted the religious minorities, specifically Muslims. Some 67,000 people were arrested under The Terrorist and Disruptive Activities (Prevention) Act (TADA), but only 8,000 put on trial, and just 725 convicted. Official TADA review committees found its application untenable in all but 5,000 cases. POTA's abuse was even more appalling.

The two new laws will increase the alienation of Muslims from the Indian state given that they have been the principal victims of India's recent anti-terrorism strategy. Many Muslims are also distressed at the alacrity with which the laws were passed—in contrast with the UPA's failure to enact the promised law to punish communal violence and hate crimes.

This will make the social–political climate conducive to state terrorism, promote muscular nationalism, and create a barbed-wire mentality. These are the ingredients of a terrible national security state, much like Pakistan's or Israel's, and similar to the way the US is evolving. Nothing could be worse for our citizens' safety and our democracy's health.

7

Responding to Mumbai Terror: Need for Diplomacy and Restraint, not War*

PRAFUL BIDWAI

Ultimately, it was not superior firepower, high-tech communications, sophisticated interception methods or commando training that explains how one of the Mumbai attackers was arrested alive at Girgaum Chowpatty. The key to that spectacular feat lies in the remarkable presence of mind and great courage shown by the city's policemen in overpowering Mohammed Ajmal Amir Iman (Kasab) with nothing more than *lathi*s after his accomplice Abu Ismail was killed.

Assistant Sub-inspector Tukaram Ombale caught and held on to the barrel of Kasab's powerful gun and pounced on the man even as he took a burst of fire, allowing his colleagues to disarm and arrest him. Ombale died, but his act of exemplary bravery ensured that a key participant in the attack would live to tell the tale.

Kasab's arrest is a rare, if not unique, event in the annals of anti-terrorist operations anywhere. His interrogation has produced invaluable evidence about the preparation for the November 26 attack, and its

*This article has already been published in *The Shillong Times* on 29 December 2008.

planning and execution. Kasab must be put on trial in a scrupulously fair manner and with full respect for his right to legal defence. Maharashtra's legal aid machinery should draft a lawyer of unimpeachable competence to defend him to dispel the impression that his conviction is a foregone conclusion merely because of the attack's enormity and barbarity. His guilt must be proved beyond doubt and on the highest norms of criminal law.

After Kasab's disclosures to the police, there can be little doubt that Pakistan-based Lashkar-e-Taiba (LeT) carried out the attack after putting a large number of recruits through rigorous training and ideological–political indoctrination for almost a year. The Pakistani media has since verified Kasab's identity and home address, and interviewed his father in Faridkot village in Okara district in Pakistan's Punjab. The international community has confirmed LeT's involvement through the ban imposed on its sister organization, Jamaat-ud-Dawa, by the United Nations Security Council under Resolution 1267 pertaining to Al Qaeda/Taliban.

LeT is not just another jihadi extremist group. It has had a special relationship with Pakistan's Inter-Services Intelligence agency (ISI), which protects it. Unlike other extremist groups such as Jaish-e-Mohammed, which are Deobandi in orientation, LeT follows the Salafist doctrine and does not believe in fighting governments in Islamic countries. LeT does not actively oppose the Pakistan Army's anti-Taliban–Al Qaeda operations at the western border with Afghanistan.

It is not clear if the ISI or its 'rogue' elements were behind the Mumbai plot or gave it logistical support. But it is reasonably plain that the attackers' main motive was to provoke a military response from India, which would lead to tension and a troops build-up at the India–Pakistan border. This would create a rationale for moving 100,000 Pakistani troops from the western border—where they have faced considerable pressure from combined US–Pakistan operations since September—and redeploying them at the Indian border. Reduced pressure on Al Qaeda–Taliban fighters will allow them to regroup and eventually overrun large swathes of Afghanistan and Pakistan's tribal agency areas.

Secondarily, the Mumbai attackers' motive was to increase disaffection among Indian Muslims and provoke a possible backlash against them—to further polarize the communal divide and help extremism. Mercifully, this has not happened—despite, not because of, the Sangh Parivar. The attacks have triggered unprecedented Hindu–Muslim unity and a spirited condemnation of terrorism by an overwhelming majority of India's Muslim social and religious organizations.

If India retaliates militarily to the Mumbai attacks, it would play straight into the hands of LeT and other extremists. Letting up pressure on the Taliban at the Afghanistan border would further destabilize Pakistan, which is already in a precarious condition, to the point of unravelling its state—with potentially disastrous consequences for India.

The Indian government has done well by acting with restraint and using diplomatic rather than military means to deal with the crisis. On 11 December, External Affairs Minister Pranab Mukherjee underscored this approach in Parliament. In response to an interjection demanding an attack on Pakistan, he said, 'That is not the point. That is not the issue. I am making it quite clear that that is not the solution. Let us be very clear and frank that that is no solution.'

Let as understand the meaning of the military option, which is advocated stridently by hawkish 'strategic experts' and by Bharatiya Janata Party MPs such as Mr Arun Shourie (*The Daily Star*, 2009 [website]). Mr Shourie wants India to target Pakistan's vital installations and keep Pakistan 'preoccupied', presumably through covert action, with its 'own problems in Balochistan, in Gilgit, Baltistan and in Pakistan-occupied Kashmir'. He said: 'Not an eye for an eye; but for an eye, both eyes. For a tooth, (the) whole jaw.' In other words, disproportionately massive retaliation!

This is an insane prescription. Any India–Pakistan conflict is liable to escalate into a nuclear war. In South Asia, nuclear weapons have manifestly failed to prevent conventional war and promote sober conflict management—in Kargil, and in the scary 2002 eyeball-to-eyeball confrontation. In Nuclear Armageddon, there are no winners—only megadeaths.

Even a limited nuclear exchange will kill millions of civilians in both India and Pakistan and cause economic and environmental damage that will set us back by decades. A single Hiroshima- or Nagasaki-type bomb dropped on a big city will kill 8–20 lakh people. And India and Pakistan both have scores of such bombs, indeed even more powerful ones.

In every conceivable war-gaming scenario—and many credible ones exist—an India–Pakistan conflict has one inevitable outcome: full-scale war, in which Pakistan would not hesitate to use nuclear weapons if it fears loss of territory or outright dismemberment. This is certain to invite nuclear retaliation from India, with consequences that are too horrifying even to contemplate.

Besides, no leader, whether Prime Minister Manmohan Singh or President Asif Ali Zardari, has the moral right or political mandate to sacrifice millions of civilians (*South Asia Times*, 2008 [website]). Only communal extremists with apocalyptic visions like RSS chief K.S. Sudarshan believe that nuclear war is acceptable. He recently told an interviewer, 'Whenever the demons (Asuri powers) start dominating this planet, there is no way other than war ... I know it will not stop there. It will be a nuclear war and a large number of people will perish. But ... it is very necessary to defeat the demons and there is no other way. And let me say with confidence that after this destruction, a new world will emerge, which will be very good, free from evil and terrorism.'

It is both absurd and dangerous to imagine that the threat of war can compel Pakistan into acting decisively against extremist groups. Indeed, it will respond more irresponsibly and with greater bellicosity. Its military leadership probably deludes itself that it can hold its own against India for a prolonged period with the arms it has stockpiled from the aid given by the US.

The idea of 'surgical strikes' against terrorist training camps is equally harebrained. LeT camps are makeshift affairs, and hence poor candidate-targets for strikes. Any strike, however 'limited', will invite armed conflict, whose effects cannot be contained. Pakistan is not Saddam Hussein's Iraq, which the US could attack without fear of resistance because it crippled all military communications. Even covert operations, which will require the creation of a new monster—'India's own ISI'—will trigger military escalation, with terrible consequences.

However, there are alternatives. Dr Manmohan Singh outlined in a two-pronged approach: galvanizing international opinion for effective action against terrorism, and persisting with diplomatic pressure on Pakistan. Domestically, he also promised radical reform of internal security arrangements. External pressure, especially through the US and UK, has already led to some tangible results in the shape of a ban on JuD. But India must develop a broader multilateral approach to avert getting drawn into Washington's parochial plans for the region.

The best multilateral strategy would be to press Pakistan through UN Security Council Resolution 1373, under which sanctions can be imposed on a state that fails to 'deny safe haven to those who finance, plan, support, or commit terrorist acts...' and violates its duty to 'refrain from providing ... support ... to entities or persons involved in terrorist acts...'.

Bilaterally, India can achieve a great deal by sharing with, and confronting, Pakistan with incontrovertible evidence about LeT's role in the Mumbai attacks, and acting demonstrably to defuse suspicions about its own covert operations in Balochistan and Afghanistan.

While revamping India's internal security system, the Singh government should have followed the sage advice of Chief Justice K.G. Balakrishnan against 'increasing governmental surveillance over citizens' and using 'questionable methods such as permitting indefinite detention of terror suspects ... coercive interrogation techniques and the denial of the right to fair trial', and his plea for 'substantive due process'.

Regrettably, the government has done the very opposite by having a law passed which replicates most of the obnoxious provisions, including detention without charges for 180 days, of the discredited, draconian Prevention of Terrorism Act—except for making confessions to the police admissible as evidence. The National Investigative Agency Act too is full of flaws, including overcentralization of powers, and their illegitimate extension to areas affected by insurgency and left-wing extremism. These acts must be undone.

Websites

1. http://www.thedailystar.net/magazine/2009/01/01/food.htm, accessed on 2 January 2009.
2. http://www.southasiatimes.com.au/news/commentary-responding-to-the-mumbai-carnage/, accessed on 23 December 2008.

8

Mumbai under Siege*

YOGINDER SIKAND

O ye who believe! stand out firmly for God, as witnesses to fair dealing, and let not the hatred of others to you make you swerve to wrong and depart from justice. Be just: that is next to piety: and fear God. For God is well-acquainted with all that ye do.

(The Quran, Surah Al-Maida: 8)

Numerous theories are doing the rounds about the dastardly terrorist assault on Mumbai. The dominant view, based on what is being suggested by the media, is that this is the handiwork of the dreaded Pakistan-based self-styled Islamist and terrorist outfit Lashkar-e-Taiba, which, ever since it was ostensibly proscribed by the Government of Pakistan some years ago, has adopted the name of Jamaat ud-Dawah. This might well be the case, for the Lashkar has been responsible for numerous such terrorist attacks in recent years, particularly in Kashmir.

The Lashkar is the military wing of the Markaz Dawat wal Irshad, an outfit floated by a section of the Pakistani Ahl-e Hadith, a group with close affiliations to the Saudi Wahhabis. It has its headquarters at

---

*The article has been published in Global Research on 30 November 2008 and is available online at islampeaceandjustice.blogspot.com.

the town of Muridke in the Gujranwala district in Pakistani Punjab. The Markaz was established in 1986 by two Pakistani university professors, Hafiz Muhammad Saeed and Zafar Iqbal. They were assisted by Abdullah Azam, a close aide of Osama bin Laden, who was then associated with the International Islamic University in Islamabad. Funds for setting up the organization are said to have come from Pakistan's dreaded official secret services agency, the Inter Services Intelligence (ISI). From its inception, it is thus clear, the Lashkar had the support of the Pakistani establishment.

The Lashkar started out as a paramilitary organization to train warriors to fight the Soviets in Afghanistan. Soon it spawned dozens of camps across Pakistan and Afghanistan for this purpose. Militants produced at these centres have played a major role in armed struggles, first in Afghanistan, and then in Bosnia, Chechnya, Kosovo, the southern Philippines and Kashmir.

Like other radical Islamist groups, the Lashkar sees Islam as an all-embracing system. It regards Islam as governing all aspects of personal as well as collective life, in the form of the shariah. For the establishing of an Islamic system, it insists, an 'Islamic state' is necessary, which will impose the shariah as the law of the land. If, the official website of the Lashkar announces, such a state were to be set up and all Muslims were to live strictly according to 'the laws that Allah has laid down', then, it is believed, 'they would be able to control the whole world and exercise their supremacy'. And for this, as well as to respond to the oppression that it claims that Muslims in large parts of the world are suffering, it insists that all Muslims must take to armed jihad. Armed jihad must continue, its website announces, 'until Islam, as a way of life, dominates the whole world and until Allah's law is enforced everywhere in the world.

The subject of armed jihad runs right through the writings and pronouncements of the Lashkar and is, in fact, the most prominent theme in its discourse. Indeed, its understanding of Islam may be seen as determined almost wholly by this preoccupation, so much so that its reading of Islam seems to be a product of its own political project, thus effectively ending up equating Islam with terror. Being born as a result of war in Afghanistan, war has become the very raison d'être of the Lashkar, and its subsequent development has been almost entirely determined by this concern. The contours of its ideological framework are constructed in such a way that the theme of armed jihad appears as the central element of its project. In the writings and speeches of Lashkar spokesmen jihad appears as violent conflict (*qital*) waged against 'unbelievers' who are said to be responsible for the oppression of the Muslims. Indeed, the Lashkar projects it as the one of the most central tenets of Islam, although it has traditionally not been included as one of the 'five pillars' of the faith. Thus, its website claims that 'There is so much emphasis on this subject that some commentators and scholars of the Quran have remarked that the topic of the Quran is jihad.' Further, a Lashkar statement declares, 'There is consensus of opinion among researchers of the Quran that no other action has been explained in such great detail as jihad.'

In Lashkar discourse, jihad against non-Muslims is projected as a religious duty binding on all Muslims today. Thus the Lashkar's website claims that a Muslim who has 'never intended to fight against the disbelievers [...] is not without traces of hypocrisy'. Muslims who have the capacity to participate or assist in the jihad but do not do so are said to 'be living a sinful life'. Not surprisingly, therefore, the Lashkar denounces all Muslims who do not agree with its pernicious and grossly distorted version of Islam and its hideous misinterpretation of jihad—Sufis, Shias, Barelvis and so on—as being 'deviants' or outside the pale of Islam or even in league with 'anti-Islamic forces'. The Lashkar promises its activists that they would receive great rewards, both in this world and in the hereafter, if they were to actively struggle in the path of jihad. Not only would they be guaranteed a place in heaven, but they would also 'be honoured in this world', for jihad, it claims, is also 'the way that solves financial and political problems'.

Astoundingly bizarre though it is, the Markaz sees itself as engaged in a global jihad against the forces of 'disbelief', stopping at nothing short of aiming at the conquest of the entire world. As Nazir Ahmed, in-charge of the public relations department of the Lashkar, once declared, through the so-called jihad that the Lashkar has launched, 'Islam will be dominant all over the world.' This global war is seen as a solution to all the ills and oppression afflicting all Muslims, and it is claimed that 'if we want to live with honour and dignity, then we have to return back to jihad'. Through jihad, the Lashkar website says, 'Islam will be supreme throughout the world.'

In Lashkar discourse, its self-styled jihad against India is regarded as nothing less than a war between two different and mutually opposed ideologies: Islam, on one hand, and Hinduism, on the other. It tars all Hindus with the same brush, as supposed 'enemies of Islam'. Thus, Hafiz Muhammad Saeed, Lashkar chief, declares, 'In fact, the Hindu is a mean enemy and the proper way to deal with him is the one adopted by our forefathers, who crushed them by force. We need to do the same.'

India is a major target for the Lashkar's terrorists. According to Hafiz Muhammad Saeed, 'The jihad is not about Kashmir only. It encompasses all of India.' Thus, the Lashkar sees its self-styled jihad as going far beyond the borders of Kashmir and spreading through all of India. Its final goal, it says, is to extend Muslim control over what is seen as having once been Muslim land, and, hence, to be brought back under Muslim domination, creating what the Lashkar terms as 'the Greater Pakistan by dint of jihad'. Thus, at a mammoth congregation of Lashkar supporters in November 1999, Hafiz Muhammad Saeed thundered, 'Today I announce the break-up of India, Inshallah. We will not rest until the whole of India is dissolved into Pakistan.'

The Lashkar, so say media reports, has been trying to drum up support among India's Muslims, and it may well be that it has managed to find a few recruits to its cause among them. If this is the case, it has probably been prompted by the fact of mounting murderous Hindutva-inspired anti-Muslim pogroms across the country, often abetted by agencies of the state, which has taken a toll of several thousand innocent lives. The fact that no semblance of justice has been delivered in these cases and that the state has not taken any measure to reign in Hindutva terrorism adds further to the deep-seated despondency and despair among many Indian Muslims. This might well be used by self-styled Islamist terror groups, such as the Lashkar, to promote their own agenda. Obviously, therefore, in order to counter the grave threat posed by terror groups such as the Lashkar, the Indian state needs to tackle the menace of Hindutva terror as well, which has now assumed the form of full-blown fascism. Both forms of terrorism feed on each other, and one cannot be tackled without taking on the other as well.

Mercifully, and despite the denial of justice to them, the vast majority of the Indian Muslims have refused to fall into the Lashkar's trap. The flurry of anti-terrorism conferences that have recently been organized by important Indian Islamic groups is evidence of the fact that they regard the Lashkar's perverse understanding of Islam as being wholly anti-Islamic and as a perversion of their faith. These voices urgently need to be promoted, for they might well be the most effective antidote to Lashkar propaganda. Numerous Indian Islamic scholars I know and have spoken to insist that the Lashkar's denunciation of all non-Muslims as 'enemies of Islam', its fomenting of hatred towards Hindus and India and its understanding of jihad are a complete misrepresentation of Islamic teachings. They bitterly critique its call for a universal Caliphate as foolish wishful thinking.

And they are unanimous that, far from serving the cause of the faith they claim to espouse, groups like the Lashkar have done the most heinous damage to the name of Islam, and are to blame, to a very large extent, for mounting Islamophobia globally.

At the same time as fingers of suspicion are being pointed at the Lashkar for being behind the recent Mumbai blasts, other questions are being raised in some circles. The significant fact that Hemant Karkare, the brave Anti-Terrorism Squad (ATS) chief who was killed in the terrorist assault, had been investigating the role of Hindutva terrorist groups in blasts in Malegoan and elsewhere and had received threats for this has not gone un-noticed. Nor has the related fact that the assault on Mumbai happened soon after disturbing revelations began pouring in of the role of Hindutva activists in terror attacks in different parts of India. That the attack on Mumbai has led to the issue of Hindutva-inspired terrorism now being totally sidelined is also significant.

And then there is a possible Israeli angle that some are raising. Thus, the widely-read Mumbai-based tabloid *Mid Day*, in an article about a building where numerous militants were holed up titled 'Mumbai Attack: Was Nariman House the Terror Hub?' states:

The role that Nariman House is coming to play in this entire attack drama is puzzling. Last night, residents ordered close to 100 kilograms of meat and other food, enough to feed an army or a bunch of people for twenty days. Shortly thereafter, the ten odd militants moved in, obviously, indicating that

the food and meat was ordered, keeping their visit in mind,
another cop added.

'One of the militants called up a television news channel and voiced his demands today, but, interestingly, when he was asked where are they all holed him, he said at the Israeli owned Nariman House and they are six of them here', one of the investigating cops said. Since morning, there has been exchange of gun fire and the militants seem well equipped to counter the cops fire. To top it, they have food and shelter. One wonders [if] they have the support of the residents, a local Ramrao Shanker said.

A Mossad/Israeli hand in the affair might seem far-fetched to some, but not so to others, who point to the role of Israeli agents in destabilizing a large number of countries as well as possibly operating within some radical Islamist movements, such as a group in Yemen styling itself 'Islamic Jihad', said to be responsible for the bombing of the American Embassy in Sanaa, and which is said to have close links with the Israeli intelligence. Some have raised the question if the Mossad or even the CIA might not be directly or otherwise instigating some disillusioned Muslim youth in India, Pakistan or elsewhere to take to terror by playing on Muslim grievances, operating through existing Islamist groups or spawning new ones for this purpose.

If this charge is true—although this remains to be conclusively established—the aim might be to further radicalize Muslims so as to provide further pretext for American and Israeli assaults on Islam and Muslim countries. The fact that the CIA had for years been in very close contact with the Pakistani ISI and radical Islamist groups in Pakistan is also being raised in this connection. The possible role of such foreign agencies of being behind some terror attacks that India has witnessed in recent years to further fan anti-Muslim hatred and also to weaken India is also being speculated on in some circles.

Whether all this is indeed true needs to be properly investigated. But the fact remains that it appears to be entirely in the interest of the Israeli establishment and powerful forces in America to create instability in India, fan Hindu–Muslim strife, even to the point of driving India and Pakistan to war with each other, and thereby drag India further into the deadly embrace of Zionists and American imperialists.

In other words, irrespective of who is behind the deadly attacks on Mumbai, it appears to suit the political interests and agendas of multiple and equally pernicious political forces—Islamist and Hindu radicals, fired by a hate-driven Manichaean vision of the world—but also global imperialist powers that seem to be using the attacks as a means to push India even deeper into their suicidal axis.

9
Handling Queries: Democratic Responses—Antulay Remarks and the Aftermath*

RAM PUNIYANI

The tragic terror attack on the city of Mumbai (November 2008) has shaken not only the people of city but also the whole nation. It is not the first time that terror attacks have taken place in this city. The first major one was seen in the aftermath of Mumbai carnage of 1992–93. The investigation of this blast showed that the terrorists took advantage of the gross injustices done to Muslim minority and lured a small section of them to execute their dastardly designs. Then in the aftermath of Gujarat carnage again one witnessed the blasts. The tragic happenings of Gujarat had incited this reaction. This time around 26 November 2008, there is no immediate provocation, but the role of Al Qaeda type elements is clear. What is puzzling this time around is that the attack came at a time when the investigation being done by Maharashtra ATS into Malegaon blast was leading to certain impeccable findings of the involvement of Hindutva elements. This was resulting in a hostile reaction to the ATS chief who was doing a thorough

*This article has been published earlier in Countercurrents.org.

professional job. He was being abused and criticized by the people like Advani and Modi for being *deshdrohi* (anti-national). Pune Police had also received a death threat for him from an anonymous caller just couple of days ahead of the terror attack.

After this tragedy many a versions of death of Karkare and his two colleagues came forward. The first one was that he has been killed at Taj, second one saying the death occurred in the lane near Cama Hospital and yet another one saying that he was killed while sitting in the vehicle. In this context many doubts were raised by some social activists and later by the Union Minister for Minorities Mr A.R. Antulay. His statement that 'superficially they (the terrorists) had no reason to kill Karkare. Whether he (Karkare) was a victim of terrorism or terrorism plus something, I do not know', implying that a thorough probe into his death should be undertaken to clear the mist around his death. This does not imply any finger pointing but a mere doubt, which is lurking in the minds of many.

This statement followed a vicious attack on him by many, especially by the Hindu right wing and a section of media. While many felt that the idea was to ensure that truth comes out, the others felt that he should not only be sacked from his post but a case of treason be launched against him. While few voices like those of Digvijay Singh came to support Antulay statement and Maharashtra Assembly speaker Baba Saheb Kupekar said that since Maharashtra government is setting up a probe into the allegations of negligence of the top level police officers, that committee can very well probe the death of Hemant Karkare as well.

The degree of hostile reaction to some doubt raised and need for unearthing truth in a democratic society should be taken seriously. Why and who is afraid of truth coming out? Strangely we seem to have various types of reactions which have lot of political tinge than elements of reason. One of this is to ignore some events and facts which go against the social common sense and the interests of dominant political streams. One such example is the blasts which took place in Nanded in the house of RSS worker in which two Bajrang Dal workers died while making bombs (April, 2006). While some channels can work overtime to put out the visuals of events with potential of sensationalism, this particular incident was literally blocked by large section of media. No doubt few papers and channels carried it but it remained a marginal story. Then the events of blasts in front of Mecca Masjid in Hyderabad were also attributed to the usual Jihadi elements, many of them arrested/tortured to the extreme. The blast and the tragedy was news. Later when they got released for the lack of any evidence, that was neither news nor a time to introspect as to why the wrong people are being caught, or to think if there is a need to review the line of investigation in the cases of blasts? Here the media shapes popular perception and the investigating authorities remained stuck to the old theory, terrorists are Muslims. So by overlooking the crucial news/event, a valuable lead was suppressed, the proper unearthing of which might have led to prevention of some attacks later.

The second form of reaction is from vested political elements and section of media which flows with the tide. Once Maharashtra ATS could lay its hands on the motorcycle used by terrorists in Malegaon blast, the investigation shifted to Sadhvi Pragya Singh Thakur, Swami Dayanand, Lt. Col. Prasad Purohit and Retd Major Upadhyay. This investigation being conducted with professionalism came for scathing attack from Hindutva elements that went on to intimidate the ATS officer to the extent that he went for moral support and counseling to the one of the most forthright police officers, Julio Reibero. Mr Reibero in his article in *Times of India* tells us the pressure Karkare was going through while doing his professional duty. Shiv Sena not only organized for legal support for Sadhvi and Company but also its mouthpiece *Saamana* went on to write, 'We will declare all names and addresses of policemen on Malegaon case, the people will take action. This is nothing but a ploy to defame Hindutva by people in the ATS who have taken supari (contract) of this. On such officers we spit, we spit.'

In this context all those trying to strive for truth are also being labelled with choicest abuses. Any raising of question about the investigation, the narration of incidents comes to be branded as being pro-Pakistan and anti-India. One is not arguing against India or for Pakistan, one is trying to see the real picture of things that will strengthen India. Can a hollow shell full of falsity be the base of the democratic Indian state? More we try to smoothen the knots more are we will be trying to ensure that Indian society becomes better. In this jingoism war, against Pakistan is the rash demand, quenching the instant anger generated due to terror attack. One has to see such oppressive outburst like the ones we have seen from Advani and company which are not in sync with the building of a harmonious atmosphere and justice to all. All the legal provisions at our command need to be marshaled to see that the work initiated by the likes of Karkare is not allowed to be stifled.

What does one make of the ignoring crucial leads in the first place and then reacting angrily, with such passion to the innocuous demands of a probe? This burst of pseudo nationalism needs to be understood. It is the one which wants to intimidate the voice of reason and is primarily trying to stifle the democratic space. In Antulay's case he is also being hurled abuses by the same section, labelling him as Pakistan supporter and what not. It's time our columnists remember that in democracy the people have full right to express their opinions and doubts. As a matter of fact those hysterically browbeating against those raising doubts are the ones who are undermining the nation's Constitution. Definitely the most befitting tribute to the officers, who have laid down their lives while protecting the society from the insane acts of terror, is to ensure that the truth of their death comes out and that Malegaon probe goes on properly.

10

The Mumbai Terror Attacks: Need for a Thorough Investigation*

RAVEENA HANSA

In all the confusion and horror generated by the ghastly terrorist attacks in Bombay, a dimension which has not received the attention it deserves are the circumstances surrounding the death of Anti-Terrorist Squad (ATS) Chief Hemant Karkare and two of his colleagues, encounter specialist Vijay Salaskar and Additional Commissioner of Police Ashok Kamte. The major pattern of operations involved well-organized attacks on a few high-profile sites in Colaba—the Taj, Oberoi and Trident Hotels, and the less-known Nariman House—while a parallel set of operations was centred on Victoria Terminus or VT (now known as Chhatrapati Shivaji Terminus or CST) station, Cama Hospital and the Metro Cinema, in the middle of which is the police headquarters where Karkare worked. The latter is an area where foreigners are much less likely to be found.

Why is a Proper Investigation Crucial?

Hemant Karkare was engaged in unearthing a terror network with characteristics which had not been

*This article was earlier published in Countercurrents.org on 8 December 2008.

seen so far. The investigation started by tracing the motorcycle used to plant bombs in Malegaon in September 2008 to a Hindu Sadhvi, Pragya Singh Thakur; it later uncovered a cellphone conversation between her and Ramji, the man who planted the bombs, in which she asked why more people had not been killed. For the first time, the Indian state was conducting a thorough professional probe into a terror network centred on Hindu extremist organizations with huge ramifications, some leading into military and bomb-making training camps and politicized elements in the army, others to religious figures like the Sadhvi and Dayanand Pandey, and yet others to organizations and political leaders affiliated to the BJP. These revelations confirmed an earlier enquiry by the ATS which had linked Hindu extremist groups to several terrorist attacks in Maharashtra, but had never been followed up.

One of the most potentially explosive discoveries was that a serving army officer, Lt. Col. Srikant Purohit, had procured 60 kg of RDX from government supplies, some of which was used in the terrorist attack on the Samjhauta Express (the India–Pakistan 'Understanding' train) in February 2007, in which 68 people were killed, the majority of them Pakistanis. Initially, militants of Lashkar-e-Taiba and other Islamist terror groups had been accused of carrying out the attack, but no evidence against them had been found.

The hostility generated by this investigation was enormous, with allegations (refuted by medical examinations) that the suspects had been tortured and that Karkare was being used as a political tool, and demands that the ATS team should be changed. Chief Minister of Gujarat Narendra Modi and BJP prime ministerial candidate L.K. Advani accused him of being a '*deshdrohi*' or traitor, a charge that in India carries a death penalty; the Shiv Sena offered legal aid to those accused of the terrorist attack, and an editorial in its mouthpiece *Saamna* threatened that 'the people will take action' against the ATS officers involved in the Malegaon blast probe, adding that 'on such officers we spit, we spit'! In an interview shortly before he died, Karkare admitted he was hurt by the campaign against him. On 26 November, just before the terrorist attack, the police in Pune received a call from an anonymous caller saying in Marathi that Karkare would be killed in a bomb blast within two or three days.

Just as attitudes to Karkare in society at large were polarized, with some admiring him as a hero—one Maulana went so far as to call him a 'massiha (messiah) of Muslims', an amazing tribute from a Muslim to a Hindu—while others hated him as a traitor worthy of death, attitudes within the police force too were polarized. For example, dismissed encounter specialist Sachin Vaze (who with three colleagues was charged with murder, criminal conspiracy, destruction of evidence and concealment of the dead body in the case of Khwaja Yunus shortly before the terrorist attack) was a member of the Shiv Sena, and was actively engaged in the campaign against Karkare and in support of the Malegaon blast accused.

Hard Evidence or Pulp Fiction?

Given this background, and reports that are riddled with inconsistencies, it is not surprising that many residents of Bombay are asking questions about the exact circumstances of the death of Hemant Karkare and his colleagues. The earliest reports, presumably relayed from the police via the media, said that Karkare had been killed at the Taj, and Salaskar and Kamte at Metro. If this was not true, why were we told this? And why was the story later changed? Was it because it conflicted with eye-witness accounts? In the early hours of the 27th, under the heading 'ATS Chief Hemant Karkare Killed: His Last Pics', IBNLive showed footage first of Karkare putting on a helmet and bullet-proof vest, then cut to a shootout at Metro, where an unconscious man who looks like Karkare and wearing the same light blue shirt and dark trousers (but without any blood on his shirt or the terrible wounds we saw on his face at his funeral) is being pulled into a car by two youths in saffron shirts. The commentary says that Karkare 'could well have fallen prey to just indiscriminate, random firing by the cops', and also reports that there were *two* vehicles, a Toyota Qualis and Honda City, from which the occupants were firing indiscriminately (IBNLive, 2008).

Later we were given two accounts of the killings where the venue was shifted to a deserted lane without cameras or eye-witnesses. The first account was by the lone terrorist captured alive, claiming to be A.A. Kasab from Faridkot in Pakistan and a member of the terrorist group Lashkar-e-Taiba. According to him, just two gunmen, he and Ismail Khan (also from Pakistan), first attacked VT station, where they sprayed bullets indiscriminately. (Around 58 people were killed there, over one-third of them Muslims, and many more might have been killed if the announcer, Mr Zende, had not risked his life to direct passengers to safety.) They then went to Cama, a government hospital for women and children used mainly by the poor. Initially, according to the police, Kasab claimed he and Ismail had killed Karkare, Salaskar and Kamte (MSN News, 2008a). Later, in his 'confession', he claimed that while coming out of the hospital, he and Ismail saw a police vehicle passing and hid behind a bush; then another vehicle passed them and stopped some distance away. A police officer got out and started firing at them, hitting Kasab on the hand so that he dropped his AK-47, but his companion opened fire on the officers in the car until they stopped firing. There were three bodies in the vehicle, which Khan removed, and then drove off in it with Kasab (Bulletmani's Weblog, 2008).

The other account is by police constable Arun Jadhav. According to him, Karkare, Salaskar, Kamte, a driver and four police constables including himself were driving down the alley from VT to the back entrance of Cama (barely a five-minute drive) in their Toyota Qualis to check on injured police officer Sadanand Date, when two gunmen emerged from behind trees by the left side of the road and sprayed the vehicle with bullets, killing all its inmates except Jadhav. They then dragged out the three officers, hijacked the vehicle, drove to Metro junction and then

Mantralaya in South Bombay, abandoned it when a tyre burst, and grabbed another car (*Expressindia*, 2008). According to police accounts, they then drove to Girgaum, where Kasab was injured and arrested and his companion killed (Shenoy, 2008).

These accounts raise more questions than they answer. Kasab claimed that a band of 10 terrorists landed and split up into twos, going to various destinations, he and his companion going to VT. He said they wanted to blow up the Taj, as in the attack on the Marriott in Islamabad; yet we are told that only 8 kg of RDX were found at the Taj, and even that was not used; contrast this with 600 kg of RDX and TNT used to blow up the Marriott: could they really have expected to blow up the Taj? How and why did the invaders from the sea plant bombs in taxis, one of which went off in Dockyard Road and another in Vile Parle, 25 kilometres away? He said that the terrorists planned to use their hostages as a means of escape, yet there was no attempt at any such negotiations; at other times, he said, on the contrary, that they had been instructed to fight to the death (Blakely, 2008). He said he was a labourer from Faridkot near Multan and only studied up to Class IV, but it was reported that he spoke fluent English. Several people have pointed out that the pictures of him in VT show him wearing a saffron wrist-band, a Hindu custom, and police later revealed that he could not recite a single verse from the Koran, which any child growing up in a Muslim family would have been able to do. A thoughtful article on the soc.culture.jewish group argued that the terrorists were not Muslims but mercenaries, given their appearance and behaviour (especially their reported consumption of alcohol and drugs), pointing out that they did not need to disguise themselves, since Muslims who look like Muslims are plentiful in Bombay, and would not attract undue attention (soc.culture.jewish, 2008).

During his interrogation, Kasab said that he and eight of the operatives had done a reconaissance trip to Bombay a few months prior to the attack, pretending to be students and renting a room at Colaba market, which is close to Nariman House (*MSN News*, 2008b). It is extremely hard for Pakistani nationals to get Indian visas, and they are kept under close surveillance by the police; it is also most unlikely that the Indian immigration authorities would be fooled by forged passports of another country. In that case, the Indian immigration authorities would have visa applications of nine of the terrorists including Kasab, and could match the photographs in them to those of the terrorists. Later, Kasab changed his story and said that the team who carried out reconnaisance was different from the team who had carried out the attacks.

The events in VT and Cama and the back lane also put a question mark over his story. According to witnesses, two gunmen started firing at the mainline terminus in VT at 21.55 on Wednesday night (Gaikwad, 2008a), but at precisely the same time, according to CCTV footage, two gunmen began an assault on the suburban terminus (Allvoices.com, 2008). If the first account is true, there were four gunmen at the station: where did the other two come from, and where did they go? We were shown video footage, claiming to be CCTV but without the timeline of normal CCTV footage, of Kasab and Khan wandering around the parking lot near the mainline terminus. This surely could not be before the shootout, since the station is completely deserted; and after the shootout, Kasab and Khan are supposed to have escaped via the footbridge from Platform 1 of the suburban station on the other side of VT: this, again, suggests there were four gunmen. How could Kasab possibly have been able to identify Karkare, Salaskar and Kamte in a dark alley in the dead of night according to Kasab's first story? According to his later confession, a police officer got out of the vehicle and started firing first, injuring him; did Khan really manage to kill all the rest by himself?

Witnesses in Cama hospital say the terrorists there spoke fluent Marathi, and this report in two Marathi papers (*Maharashtra Times*, 2008; Hameed, 2008) has been confirmed. The gunmen killed two guards in uniform, spared a third, who was in civilian dress and begged for his life saying he was the husband of a patient, demanded water from an employee in the staff quarters and then killed him. They then appear to have made a beeline for the 6th floor (which was empty) and the terrace, taking with them the liftman, Tikhe (Sidebar, 2008). Fifteen to thirty minutes later, six to eight policemen arrived, and another employee took them up to the 6th floor. The policemen threw a piece of steel up to the terrace, whereupon Tikhe came running down and told them there were two terrorists on the terrace. A fierce gun-battle ensued for 30 to 45 minutes, in which ACP Sadanand Date was injured. Panic-stricken patients and staff in the maternity ward on the 5th floor barricaded the door; nurses instructed the women to breast-feed their babies to keep them quiet, and one woman, who was in the middle of labour, was told to hold back the birth; but they were not invaded (Gaikwad, 2008b). Eventually, the gunmen appear to have escaped, it is not clear how. If they were Kasab and Khan, then these two must have been fluent Marathi speakers. And why would they have taken up positions on the terrace? Was it because it overlooked the lane in which Karkare, Salaskar and Kamte were later supposedly killed?

Jadhav's testimony is equally dubious. In his first account, Jadhav said Karkare was in the second row of the Qualis, while in the second account he was supposed to be in the front row with Kamte (Kher, 2008). In the second account, Salaskar was initially sitting behind the driver, but then asked the driver to slow down and got behind the wheel himself: is it plausible that an experienced encounter specialist would deliberately make himself into a sitting duck like this when they were in hot pursuit of terrorists? In the first account they were supposed to be going to check up on their injured colleague Sadanand Date, but in the second were supposed to be looking for a red car in which they had been told the gunmen were travelling. If the report about the red car was a decoy to lure them into an ambush, it is important to know who told them that the terrorists were in a red car. If the gunmen were firing from the left side, as Jadhav claimed, how was Karkare hit three times in the chest while Jadhav himself got two bullets in his right arm? In fact, the only vegetation in the part of the lane where there is evidence of a gun-battle is on the right side, and is pinned to the wall by chest-high wire netting; it would be necessary to climb over the netting to hide behind it, and climb over again to come out: impossible under the circumstances. Witnesses say only two bodies were found at the spot next morning: what happened to the third officer? Who were the three constables killed?

How did two terrorists manage to kill six police personnel, including Karkare and Kamte (who he said were armed with AK-47s) and Salaskar, an encounter specialist, when one terrorist was later captured and the other killed by policemen armed only with two rifles and lathis? Assistant Police Inspector Ombale was killed in that encounter, but his colleagues survived.

There was also an intriguing report in DNA on 28 November saying that Anand Raorane, a resident of a building opposite Nariman House, heard sounds of celebration from the terrorists there when the news of Karkare getting killed was flashed on TV: why would terrorists from Pakistan, where Karkare's Samjhauta revelations had been welcomed, rejoice at his death? The same report quoted a resident of Nariman House and a local shopkeeper who said that the terrorists had purchased large quantities of food and liquor before the attack, suggesting that more than two of them were planning to occupy the place for a long time (Sharma, 2008). Another DNA report, on

2 December, said that Sub-inspector Durgude, who had been posted in front of St Xavier's College, between the front of Cama Hospital and the exit point of the back lane onto Mahapalika Road, saw two young men whom he took to be students and called out to warn them that there was firing at Cama. When they ignored him, he approached them, upon which one of them turned an AK-47 on him and killed him (Dixit, 2008). If Kasab and Khan were in front of St Xavier's, who was firing inside Cama? Eye-witnesses in St Xavier's saw a man shot and lying on the pavement in front of the college around 12.30 a.m., while about three gunmen stood over him: who was that? Various reports said that two to eight terrorists were captured alive. Now there is only one in police custody: what happened to the other(s)?

A careful scrutiny of all the reports available so far suggests, to this writer anyway, that the killing of Karkare and his colleagues was a premeditated act, executed by his self-proclaimed enemies, some of whom had prior intelligence of the attack on the hotels and planned their own attack to coincide with it. The operation in Cama, in particular, seems to have had the sole objective of ambushing Karkare. A.R. Antulay's demand for a probe into the killing was widely supported, even though the same parties who were earlier vilifying and threatening Karkare responded by baying for Antulay's blood. P. Chidambaram's clarification that it was by chance that Karkare, Salaskar and Kamte happened to be travelling in the same vehicle does not explain any of the other anomalies: why did the terrorists go into Cama? If they were intending to slaughter people ruthlessly, as they did in VT, why did they desist—did they have a sudden crisis of conscience? If they intended to create a hostage crisis, why did they go to the 6th floor and terrace, where there were no patients or staff? On the other hand, if they were looking for a getaway vehicle, wouldn't they have been more likely to find it on the road than on the terrace of Cama? How did these Pakistanis learn to speak Marathi so fluently? And are we really expected to believe that they could defy the laws of nature by being in two places at the same time, engaged in a shootout at Cama while at the same time gunning down Sub-inspector Durgude outside St Xavier's?

The Objective: Shutting Down Terrorist Networks

These are just a few of the numerous questions being asked by vigilant Bombayites who find themselves thoroughly dissatisfied with the information that has been doled out. These are citizens who understand that their security depends on identifying Islamist terrorist networks in Pakistan and shutting them down, but feel it is equally important to identify and shut down Hindutva terrorist networks in India, which have been responsible for the majority of terrorist attacks in Maharashtra, and possibly the whole country, in the last five years. Why are they so cynical about the possibility of a genuine professional investigation? The answer is that we have too much bitter experience of investigations in which innocent people (usually Muslim youth) are rounded up, tortured and even killed, while the real culprits are allowed to go free. Interpol chief Robert Noble's amazing revelation on 23 December that India had not shared any information about the terrorists with it, despite its offer to use Interpol's extensive resources to assist in the investigation, can only fuel the suspicion that the information dished out by the police to the public via the media is not of a quality that would be acceptable to a truly professional police agency (*ABC News,* 2008). Karkare broke with this dismal record, but now he is dead. When a person who has been vilified, slandered and threatened with death is killed in suspicious circumstances, it is imperative that a proper investigation should be carried out soon, before too much evidence can be manufactured and/or destroyed. If Kasab aka Iman disappears or is assassinated like Lee Harvey Oswald, or is executed, that would be further evidence of a conspiracy.

The government and people of Pakistan have as much interest as the government and people of India in eliminating the terror networks that have killed President Asif Ali Zardari's wife Benazir Bhutto and thousands of others in both Pakistan and India. The terrorists, on the other hand, be they Islamist or Hindutva, have a common interest in destroying secularism, democracy and peace within and between the two countries. That is their precise agenda. Pakistani politicians have offered a joint investigation into the terrorist attacks, a far more sensible suggestion than the belligerent statements by some Indians accusing Pakistan of harbouring terrorists who are killing Indians. It should be obvious that a military conflict between India and Pakistan would be disastrous for both countries economically, while a nuclear war, which might ensue if extremist forces captured power in both countries, would have unthinkable consequences. If the Indo-Pakistan peace process had been halted, as L.K. Advani advocated, the terrorists would have won.

Indeed, without a joint investigation, the terrorist networks behind this outrage can never be uncovered: how else could the names and addresses in Pakistan revealed by Kasab be followed up to the satisfaction of all parties? Interpol could act as a coordinating agency, but would not be able to follow up information about the terrorists unless it is provided by the Indian authorities. The Indian government owes it to the memory of Karkare, who died fighting terrorism of all hues, to establish a credible account of exactly where, when and how he was killed, and identify his killers; unlike the well-known female TV anchor and others, who berated Antulay for 'helping Pakistan', we do not have to agree that one has to be a moron in order to be a good Indian! They also owe it to the rest of the victims, and to us, the public, who are the prime targets of all terrorist attacks, to carry out a credible investigation which identifies and puts behind bars all the mass murderers involved in this and other attacks.

References

ABC News. 2008. 'India Being Less Than Helpful with Mumbai Bombings Evidence: Interpol', 23 December. Available online at http://www.abc.net.au/news/stories/2008/12/23/2454145.htm, accessed on 15 September 2009.

Allvoices.com. 2008. 'CCTV of Chhatrapati Shivaji Terminus (SCT) Terrorist Attack at Mumbai', December. Available online at http://www.allvoices.com/contributed-news/1950266-see-cctv-of-chhatrapati-shivaji-terminus-cst-terrorist-attack-at-mumbai, accessed on 15 September 2009.

Blakely, Rhys. 2008. 'I was ordered to kill "until the last breath"', *Timesonline,* 1 December. Available online at http://www.timesonline.co.uk/tol/news/world/asia/article5262244.ece, accessed on 15 September 2009.

Bulletmani's Weblog. 2008. 'Confession and Narration of the Mumbai Terrorist Attack by a Terrorist—Exclusive', 15 December. Available online at http://bulletmani.wordpress.com/2008/12/11/confession-and-narration-of-the-mumbai-terrorist-attack-by-a-terrorist-exclusive/, accessed on 15 September 2009.

Dixit, Nikhil S. 2008. 'He Died Trying to Warn the Terrorists', *DNA,* 2 December. Available online at http://www.dnaindia.com/report.asp?newsid=1210887, accessed on 15 September 2009.

Expressindia. 2008. 'Witness Account of Karkare, Kamte and Salaskar's Death', 29 November. Available online at http://www.expressindia.com/latest-news/Witness-account-of-Karkare-Kamte-and-Salaskars-death/392181/, accessed on 15 September 2009.

Gaikwad, Rahi. 2008a. 'Retracing the CST attack', *The Hindu,* 4 December. Available online at http://www.hindu.com/2008/12/04/stories/2008120461882000.htm, accessed on 8 December 2008.

———. 2008b. 'India—Mumbai Attacks; Cama Staff Rose to Occasion', 3 December. Available online at http://spoonfeedin.blogspot.com/2008/12/india-mumbai-attackscama-staff-rose-to.html, accessed on 15 September 2009.

Hameed, Abdul. 2008. 'Mumbai Attack: Terrorists Spoke Marathi?' 29 November. Available online at http://www.twocircles.net/2008nov29/mumbai_attack_terrorists_spoke_marathi.html, accessed on 15 September 2009.

IBNLive. 2008. 'ATS Chief Hemant Karkare Killed: His Last Pics', 27 November. Available online at http://ibnlive.

The Mumbai Terror Attacks | 79

in.com/videos/79133/ats-chief-hemant-karkare-killed-his-last-pics.html, accessed on 15 September 2009.

Kher, Swatee. 2008. 'They Threw Salaskar, Kamte and Karkare's Bodies from the Vehicle', *Indian Express*, 30 November. Available online at http://www.indianexpress.com/news/they-threw-salaskar-kamte-and-karkare.../392336/, accessed on 15 September 2009.

Maharashtra Times. 2008. 'Dahashatvadyanchi "Marathi Boli"?' 28 November. Available online at http://maharashtratimes.indiatimes.com/articleshow/3767093.cms, accessed on 15 September 2009 .

MSN News. 2008a. 'Kasab confesses, says no regrets on Mumbai mayhem', 30 November 2008. Available online at http://news.in.msn.com/national/article.aspx?cp-documentid=1711188, accessed on 8 December 2008.

———. 2008b. 'Terrorists planned to sail out after attack,' 29 November. Available online at http://news.in.msn.com/national/article.aspx?cp-documentid=1710741, accessed on 8 December 2008.

Sharma, Somendra. 2008. 'Mumbai: Colaba Terrorists Have Food Stocks for Three Days,' *DNA*, 28 November. Available online at http://www.dnaindia.com/report.asp?newsid=1209852, accessed on 15 September 2009.

Shenoy, T.V.R. 2008. 'Salute the Brave Constables of D B Marg Police Station', 8 December. Available online at http://www.rediff.com/news/2008/dec/08mumterror-salute-the-brave-constables-of-d-b-marg-police-station.htm, accessed on 15 September 2009.

Sidebar. 2008. 'Hospital Staffer Recounts Escape from Terrorists', *South Asia News*, 30 November. Available online at http://www.monstersandcritics.com/news/southasia/news/article_1445785.php/SIDEBAR_Hospital_staffer_recounts_escape_from_terrorists, accessed on 15 September 2009.

Soc.culture.jewish. 2008. 'The killers were NOT Muslims', 5 December. Available online at http://groups.google.com/group/soc.culture.jewish/browse_thread/thread/9eb845cf1dbfcfa6, accessed on 15 September 2009.

11

India's Terror Dossier: Further Evidence of Conspiracy*

RAVEENA HANSA

On 5 January 2009, the Indian government handed a 69-page dossier of material stemming from the ongoing investigation into the Mumbai terrorist attacks of 26–29 November 2008 to the Pakistani government. This was subsequently made accessible to the public (*The Hindu*, 2009), so it is possible for us to examine it.

The most striking point about the dossier was its vague and unprofessional character. Enormous reliance was placed on the interrogation of the captured terrorist, Mohammed Amir Kasab, despite the fact that there was an abundance of other evidence—eyewitness accounts, CCTV and TV footage, forensic evidence, etc.—which could have been called upon to establish when, where and what exactly happened during the attacks. This gives rise to the suspicion that the interrogation was being used as a substitute for real investigation because it could be influenced by intimidation or torture, whereas other sources of evidence could not be influenced in the same way.

The account gleaned from interrogation would have been far more convincing if it had been corroborated

*This article was earlier published in Countercurrents.org on 5 January 2009.

by evidence from other sources. Thus, it seems to have been established that Kasab is from Faridkot in Pakistan, and we also know from eyewitness accounts that he was captured at Girgaum, thanks to the heroism of Assistant Sub-inspector Tukaram Ombale. But a real chargesheet would require the rest of the account supplied by Kasab to be confirmed by other evidence. For those who know Bombay, who were glued to their TV screens while the ghastly events unfolded, and who also followed reports in the print media, including Marathi newspapers, the account in the dossier just won't do.

VT station (see Google maps) opens onto Dadabhai Naoroji (DN) Road, which runs northwards parallel to the railway tracks and becomes Mohammed Ali Road; Mahapalika Marg begins in front of VT, going off DN Road to the northwest. Travelling from VT along Mahapalika Marg, one passes, on the right, the Municipal Corporation buildings, the Esplanade Metropolitan Magistrate's Court, Cama Hospital, and St Xavier's College; it then carries on to Metro Junction. The third side of the triangle is constituted by Lokmanya Tilak Marg (on which the police headquarters is located) which runs between Metro Junction and Mohammed Ali Road. However, a large part of the triangle is occupied by a police complex, including police residential quarters. Running between DN Road and Mahapalika Marg is a lane, at least part of which is named Badaruddin Tyabji Marg, which goes off DN Road opposite the middle of VT station, turns right, going past the back of the Esplanade court and Cama Hospital on the left, then some distance further passes the CID Special Branch building which houses the Foreigners' Regional Registration Office (the southernmost part of the large and sprawling police complex) on the right, turns sharp left, passes the side of St Xavier's College on the left, and exits onto Mahapalika Marg. It is important to keep this geography in mind when assessing the account in the dossier.

A Very Significant Omission

Let us follow one trail from the point where the terrorists landed. According to the dossier, all 10 terrorists landed at Badhwar Park on Cuffe Parade in an inflatable dinghy, then split into five pairs, and took taxis to their destinations. Kasab and Ismail Khan were assigned to CST station (better known as VT), and allegedly entered the station and started firing indiscriminately at 'about 21.20 hrs' (p. 5). But according to an eyewitness at VT, Bharat Patel (a chef at Re-Fresh Food Plaza which was riddled with bullet-holes), firing in the mainline station started at 9.55 p.m. (Gaikwad, 2008a). According to CCTV footage, it was at 21.55 that passengers, who had earlier been walking around normally, began running for cover in the suburban part of the station while the railway police attempted to take on the terrorists, and at 22.13 p.m., the terrorists were still in VT station (Allvoices.com, 2008). Motorman O.M. Palli said, 'I heard the last bullet sound at 10.32,' and when asked how he could be so sure of the time, replied, 'I am a motorman; I keep time by the seconds' (Gaikwad, 2008b). So why did the dossier prepone the assault by 35 minutes, when there is evidence which enables us to establish its timing far more precisely?

The dossier continues, "They left the station, crossed an over-bridge and fled into a lane towards Cama hospital. Near Cama hospital they were challenged by a police team and there was an exchange of fire. As they exited the lane, they fired on a police vehicle carrying three senior police officers and four policemen' (p. 6). The reader of this account is being asked to believe that Kasab and his colleague were involved in two encounters, presumably survived the first to be able to engage in the second, and that these encounters occurred in relatively quick succession. Prima facie, none of this sounds credible. In fact, what the dossier has done is to transpose an incident that occurred in Cama Hospital to the area just outside the hospital, in the lane at the back. What happened in Cama Hospital for Women and Children was that two 'Marathi-speaking' terrorists armed with AK-47s and grenades killed two guards and spared a third who was in civilian dress and begged for his life (*Maharashtra Times*, 2008; Hameed, 2008), and then made a beeline for the terrace of the hospital, taking the liftman Tikhe with them (Sidebar, 2008). After 15–30 minutes, a police party led by officer Sadanand Date arrived, was taken up to the 6th floor (which had no wards and was therefore empty at night) by another guard, Ghegadamal, after which a fierce battle ensued for 30–45 minutes, during which Date was seriously injured and two policemen died (Gaikwad, 2008c).

The fact that an incident took place in Cama Hospital involving two Marathi-speaking attackers, and that this was reported in the papers, would obviously be a source of embarrassment if the dossier was bent on showing that the terror attacks of late November involved only Pakistani nationals. Presumably that is why this whole sequence of events (in Cama Hospital) was omitted from the dossier. In fact, this omission raises several other questions. First and foremost, who were these Marathi-speaking terrorists, why were they in Cama Hospital, and what happened to them afterwards?

Second, and no less important, is the question asked by Minority Affairs Minister A.R. Antulay: if there was no hostage situation in the hospital, why was an officer of the rank of ATS Chief Karkare sent there, and not to the Taj, Oberoi or Nariman House, where battles would have been raging by this time. (Manoj and Chishti, 2008)? According to constable Arun Jadhav, who is the only eyewitness cited in the dossier (p. 6), Hemant Karkare and others were called to Cama only *after* Date was wounded and had to retreat, which could not have been before 23.40, and was possibly somewhat later (*Expressindia*, 2008).

This timing is corroborated by the account given by a government driver, Maruti Phad, who lived off the lane in which the officers were reportedly killed. He stated on NDTV that at 23.30 he received a call from his boss, the Medical Education Secretary, summoning him to Mantralaya. As he drove down the lane to Mahapalika Marg, there was firing, and he was hit in the hand by bullets. He had the presence of mind to duck and reverse rapidly, and when the car stopped, pretended to be dead. The last thing Mr Phad added as he concluded his account of this episode was, '*Karkare mere pichhe thha*' ('Karkare was behind me') (Wagh, 2008). Again, a proper investigation would have to reconstruct details from his eyewitness testimony. Here the suggestion seems to be that the killers of Karkare, whoever they were, were waiting at the corner outside St Xavier's College, and mistook Phad's vehicle for the one which Karkare was using.

In fact, the battle in which Karkare and his companions were reportedly killed was not at the exit of the lane but several yards before the exit, in front of the branch of Corporation Bank at the side of St Xavier's College, which bore the marks of several bullet-holes. If we accept that Kasab and Khan conducted the massacre in VT, then they would have escaped from VT station, crossed the footbridge over DN Road and run along the lane going past the back of Cama Hospital around 22.40. If they were not involved in the attack inside Cama, *what possible reason would they have for hanging around for at least an hour in a lane which is on the edge of a police complex and would have been full of cops by then due to the standoff at Cama*, when they could have hijacked any number of cars from the main road (Mahapalika Marg) and escaped? Even in the event that they had been told Karkare was a target (extremely unlikely, since Karkare's revelations regarding the Samjhauta blasts had been welcomed in Pakistan), neither they nor their handlers in Pakistan could possibly have known that he would be coming down that lane an hour later. Given all this, it seems most unlikely that they could have been the killers of the police officers and constables killed in Badaruddin Tyabji Lane. Which leaves us with the crucial question: *who killed Hemant Karkare?*

A.R. Antulay was by no means alone in raising doubts about who exactly had killed Hemant Karkare, nor were such questions raised only by Muslims. Given that leading members of the BJP and Shiv Sena had vented open hostility against Karkare and the Malegaon blast investigations, demanded that he be removed from the case and organized support for the accused, the people who had the most obvious motive for killing him were certainly not Pakistanis. Indeed, earlier on the 26th, an editorial in the Shiv Sena's *Saamna* attacked the investigation, and Karkare received a death threat (Rajesh, 2008). When someone who has been vilified and threatened with death is killed under mysterious circumstances, it is only logical to suspect those who had been conducting a campaign against him of having a hand in his death. The way the dossier constructs its narrative points in the same direction.

Other Anomalies and Omissions

According to Jadhav's original testimony, Kasab and Khan hijacked the police vehicle in which Karkare had been travelling and drove it first to Metro Junction, where they fired three rounds at journalists and police vans (*Expressindia*, 2008). There was indeed a shootout at Metro, captured on camera by a TV crew (IBN Live, 2008), but there is no mention at all of this incident in the dossier. Why not? Again, the implication is that the terrorists involved in the incident at Metro were not Kasab and Khan but members of the other group, who drove there after killing Karkare and his companions.

Second, the dossier mentions that a return journey to Pakistan was charted on the GPS instrument (pp. 22–23), yet the terrorists, unlike those who hijacked Indian Airlines Flight IC-814 to Kandahar, made no attempt to use their hostages to secure their own or anyone else's escape. If, for example, they had announced, via the e-mail connection they used to claim the attacks for the 'Deccan Mujahideen', the names of some high-profile and foreign hostages, there would have been enormous pressure on the Indian government from family, friends and governments of the hostages to get them released. The fact that there was no such attempt suggests that this was a suicide mission; in which case, why was a return journey to Pakistan charted on the GPS when no one would be returning?

Third, the intercepted calls cited in the dossier were emphatic that no Muslims should be killed (pp. 53, 54), yet in the carnage at VT station, 22 of the victims—well over one-third of the total—were Muslims (Ramani, 2008). The Walliullah family lost six members, and many of these victims would easily have been identified as Muslims from their appearance. This almost suggests that Muslims were deliberately being targeted: the exact opposite of what the Pakistani handlers had ordered! One possible explanation of this, also suggested by the fact that there were simultaneous attacks on the mainline and suburban sections of VT, is that there were two pairs of terrorists attacking the station, one of which was not from Pakistan.

Fourth, it is clear from the translations of selected intercepted calls in the dossier (Annexure VII, pp. 51–54) that the cellphones of the terrorists were the main means by which they stayed in touch with their handlers and received instructions from them. What is not mentioned is that on 6 December, two people were arrested by the Kolkata police for supplying three SIM cards for these very cellphones: Tausif Rehman and Mukhtar Ahmed. Rehman was reported to have obtained the SIM cards in the name of deceased persons and other fake IDs, while Ahmed passed them on to LeT operatives.

Initially seen as a breakthrough in the investigation, the arrests soon became an embarrassment when it was discovered that Ahmed was an Indian intelligence operative who had infiltrated LeT. This incident has been used to make the charge that the whole Mumbai terrorist attack was a 'false flag' operation masterminded by Indian, US and Israeli intelligence services (Nimmo, 2008). This seems far-fetched, but it certainly appears that something more sinister than a mere 'intelligence failure' on the part of Indian intelligence services is involved. What the SIM card episode and other reports suggest is that some parts of the Indian intelligence establishment had prior intimation that an attack was being planned. This prior intelligence was specific enough to identify seaside targets, in particular hotels. Hotel managements were in fact issued a general security alert some weeks before the attacks. Despite this, no attempt was made to prevent the attacks.

A month after the attacks, the government of Maharashtra appointed a two-member enquiry committee consisting of former Union Home Secretary Ram Pradhan and retired Indian Police Service officer V. Balachandran to investigate the occurrence of the terrorist attack and management of the ensuing crisis by the state administration. There were hopes that these professionals, as well as the court conducting the trial of Kasab, would look at the evidence in its totality, sifting the more reliable pieces of information from those which were either patently false or contrived in some way.

Conspiracy Theories versus Supernatural Explanations

Most people react negatively to conspiracy theories. It is as if, when you are a child, someone tells you that your mother or father is a criminal: the first response is denial, even if you know in your heart of hearts that there is something in the accusation. From this comes the stereotype of 'conspiracy theorists' as crackpots.

Yet there are occasions when the conspiracy theory makes sense, and it is those denying it who have to resort to supernatural explanations. A famous case is the assassination of President John F. Kennedy. The Warren Commission, set up to enquire into the assassination, came out with the theory that he was killed by a lone assassin, Lee Harvey Oswald, who was subsequently himself assassinated. But several books, as well as Oliver Stone's film *JFK*, showed that the official version rested on the assumption of three bullets fired from the same location, one of which changed direction more than once, went through President Kennedy and Governor Connally, and emerged in an almost pristine condition. Against this 'magic bullet' theory, the alternative explanation—that there was more than one assassin—sounds more plausible, especially given eyewitness accounts that there were more than three shots, and that they came from different directions. But the failure to pursue this line of investigation strongly suggests a conspiracy, and a large majority of Americans believe in it.

Closer to our time, the 9/11 Commission report gave rise to considerable criticism in the US; by November 2008, there were apparently some 150 million websites devoted to 9/11 conspiracy theories, several books had been written, and a large number of Americans believed the attack had been an 'inside job' designed to provide a pretext for military attacks on Afghanistan and Iraq.[1] (For these people, incidentally, the claim that '26/11 was India's 9/11' would mean that the Indian state is implicated in the Mumbai attacks!) It would be hard to prove that all these people are crackpots: many are scholars, pilots, architects, engineers and other professionals with specialized knowledge, as well as eyewitnesses. One of the criticisms related to the claim that it was the fire generated by the planes crashing into the WTC towers that led to their collapsing on their own footprint. Never before or since has fire led to buildings collapsing in this way, they argue, whereas this is exactly what happens when a controlled demolition takes place. They clinch the argument by referring to WTC Tower 7, which collapsed on its footprint without even being hit by a plane.

Controlled demolitions imply that explosives had been laid beforehand, and that evidence for them was covered up afterwards: that is, a conspiracy. But, like the JFK assassination, this is a case where the conspiracy theory complies with the laws of nature whereas the official version does not.

It is not necessary to allege that the government or head of state is involved in a conspiracy: it would be absurd, for example, to suspect that President Kennedy was involved in a plot to assassinate himself. All that is required is that some elements in the state are involved. So what would a conspiracy theory of the Bombay terrorist attacks look like? One hypothesis is that Hindu nationalist elements in the Indian state had fairly precise intelligence of the planned terrorist attacks in Bombay, but instead of acting to prevent them, decided to enhance them instead, by adding more terrorists to the operation at VT, putting bombs in the taxis which blew up at Dockyard Road and Vile Parle, and positioning gunmen throughout the area, including Cama and the vicinity of the Metro.

Why would they have conspired in this way? Two reasons. The first and the most pressing reason was that Hemant Karkare was rapidly uncovering just how extensive their network was, and how deeply they were implicated in a large number of terrorist attacks which had previously been attributed to Muslim jihadi groups. He had to be stopped at all costs, but an obvious murder by Hindutva terrorists could lead to a backlash against them. A terrorist attack by Pakistanis provided the perfect cover for the assassination. The second reason was that several Assembly elections were pending, and the BJP would be able to take advantage of the attack to accuse the UPA of being 'soft on terrorism'. In fact, the disappointment and dismay of BJP leaders after the election results came out was very evident, when they discovered that they had not gained as much as they hoped from the Mumbai attacks. But this disappointment was offset by the elimination of Karkare. The Minister of External Affairs, Prime Minister, Defence Minister, etc. immediately blamed 'Pakistan' for the attack, and the whole discourse of the media, which had been following the Malegaon case, shifted decisively back to 'terrorists from Pakistan'.

This 'conspiracy theory' is able to explain several things which remain unexplained in the 'official version', for example: (a) why, despite prior intelligence of the attacks, nothing was done to prevent them; (b) the Cama Hospital incident involving Marathi-speaking terrorists, and the outbreak of firing and general mayhem at Metro Junction; (c) the carnage at VT, where far more people were killed than at any other location, and the high proportion of Muslims killed there (contrary to the instructions given to the main group of terrorists) and (d) last but not least, the murder of Hemant Karkare at a time when Pakistani terrorists would only have been present at that location if time had stood still during the hour or more when the battle at Cama Hospital was raging.

Providing Justice to the Victims and Security to the Public

The main requirement for providing justice to the victims of the attack is to identify and punish all those involved in perpetrating it. This should be done in a manner that satisfies the requirements of the law. The Lockerbie case, which involved a terrorist attack on a plane over Scotland, victims from the US, UK and France, and accused from Libya, was tried by a Scottish court sitting in The Hague. A similar model would have been ideal in this case: trial by an Indian court, since the attack took place in India and most of the victims were Indian, but in The Hague, since there were also victims from 15 other countries (see p. 14 of the dossier) and the accused are from Pakistan. Given that the trial is to take place in India, it is especially important to have transparent legal proceedings that conform to international standards in order to help ensure that the case is conducted to the satisfaction of all parties, and also help to defuse the tension between Pakistan and India.

The broader aim of providing security to the public requires that members of terrorist networks in both countries should be rounded up and put behind bars. It is good that the international community is putting pressure on the government of Pakistan to do this in their country, and it is essential that this pressure should be sustained till results are achieved. As long as the Pakistan-based terror networks remain intact, further strikes cannot be ruled out, and these could have catastrophic political consequences for the subcontinent. But focusing simply on those networks will not, by itself, provide safety to the public in India. Their security in addition requires the Indian government to eliminate terrorist networks in India, including Hindutva ones. It is heartening that the ATS is proceeding with the prosecution of the Malegaon blast accused, and has presented the 4250-page chargesheet that Hemant Karkare risked his life to work on, although it remains to be seen whether convictions will follow or the accused will be acquitted on some pretext. But even if there are convictions, that is not enough; Karkare was only able to uncover the tip of the iceberg before he was struck down, and a great deal more remains to be done. If it is not, it is possible that the Hindutva terrorists may strike again, and the parties that are linked to the terrorists may use the opportunity to accuse the UPA of being 'soft on terrorism' in order to come to power. If they succeed, we could be faced with the horrific prospect of a military conflict between India and Pakistan that escalates into nuclear war.

Note

1. See, for example, 9–11 *Inside Job,* Available online at http://bushstole04.com/. Accessed online on 15 September 2009, *The 9/11 Truth Movement,* Available online at http://www.911truth.org/. Accessed online on 15 September 2009, and millions of other websites that come up if you type '9/11 truth' into Google.

References

Allvoices.com. 2008. 'CCTV of Chhatrapati Shivaji Terminus (CST) Terrorist Attack at Mumbai', December. Available online at http://www.allvoices.com/contributed-news/1950266-see-cctv-of-chhatrapati-shivaji-terminus-cst-terrorist-attack-at-mumbai, accessed on 15 September 2009.

Expressindia. 2008. 'Witness Account of Karkare, Kamte and Salaskar's Death', 29 November. Available online at http://www.indianexpress.com/news/witness-account-of-karkare-kamte-and-salaskars-death/392181/, accessed on 15 September 2009.

Gaikwad, Rahi. 2008a. 'Retracing the CST Attack', *The Hindu*, 4 December. Available online at http://www.hindu.com/2008/12/04/stories/2008120461882000.htm, accessed on 15 September 2009.

———. 2008b. 'A hero at work', *Frontline*, 20 December. Available online at http://www.hinduonnet.com/fline/fl2526/stories/20090102252602800.htm, accessed on 15 September 2009.

———. 2008c. 'India–Mumbai Attacks; Cama Staff Rose to Occasion', 3 December. Available online at http://spoonfeedin.blogspot.com/2008/12/india-mumbai-attackscama-staff-rose-to.html, accessed on 15 September 2009.

Google maps, Badaruddin Tyabji Marg, http://maps.google.com/maps?hl=en&q=badaruddin%20tyabji%20marg&um=1&ie=UTF-8&sa=N&tab=wl (the link takes you to a map of the US, and asks, 'Did you mean: Badaruddin Tyabji Marg… etc.' If you click on this link you go to the correct map.)

Hameed. Abdul. 2008. 'Mumbai Attack: Terrorists Spoke Marathi?' 29 November. Available online at http://www.twocircles.net/2008nov29/mumbai_attack_terrorists_spoke_marathi.html, accessed on 15 September 2009.

IBNLive. 2008. 'ATS Chief Hemant Karkare Killed: His Last Pics', 27 November. Available online at http://ibnlive.in.com/videos/79133/ats-chief-hemant-karkare-killed--his-last-pics.html, accessed on 15 September 2009.

Maharashtra Times. 2008. 'Dahashatvadyanchi "Marathi Boli"?' 28 November. Available online at http://maharashtratimes.indiatimes.com/articleshow/3767093.cms, accessed on 15 September 2009.

Manoj, C.G. and Chishti, Seema. 2008. 'Antulay Self-Goal: Sees a Malegaon Mystery in Karkare Mumbai Murder', *Indian Express*, 17 December. Available online at http://www.expressindia.com/latest-news/Antulay-selfgoal-sees-a-Malegaon-mystery-in-Karkare-Mumbai-murder/399670/, accessed on 15 September 2009.

Nimmo, Kurt. 2008. 'Arrest Provides More Evidence India, Israel, and the US Behind Mumbai Attacks', *PrisonPlanet*, 7 December. Available online at http://www.prisonplanet.com/arrest-provides-more-evidence-india-israel-and-the-us-behind-mumbai-attacks.html, accessed on 15 September 2009.

Rajesh, Y.P. 2008. 'Karkare's Response to a Death Threat: A "Smiley"', Expressindia, 27 November. Available online at http://www.expressindia.com/latest-news/ATS-chief-Hemant-Karkare-dies-a-heros-death/391325/, accessed on 15 September 2009.

Ramani, Srinivasan. 2008. 'Attack on "Everyday India"', *Pragoti*, 9 December. Available online at http://www.pragoti.org/node/2720, accessed on 15 September 2009.

Sidebar. 2008. 'Hospital Staffer Recounts Escape from Terrorists', *South Asia News*, 30 November. Available online at http://www.monstersandcritics.com/news/southasia/news/article_1445785.php/SIDEBAR_Hospital_staffer_recounts_escape_from_terrorists_, accessed on 15 September 2009.

The Hindu. 2009. 'Mumbai Terror Attacks—Dossier of Evidence'. Available online at http://www.hindu.com/nic/dossier.htm, accessed on 15 September 2009.

Wagh, Prachi Jawdekar. 2008. 'Mumbai driver recounts battle for survival', 6 December. Available online at http://www.ndtv.com/convergence/ndtv/mumbaiterrorstrike/Story.aspx?ID=NEWEN20080075496&type=News, accessed on 15 September 2009.

12
Terrorism, Rule of Law and Human Rights*

K.G. BALAKRISHNAN

Adherence to the constitutional principle of 'substantive due process' must be an essential part of our collective response to terrorism. Any dilution of the right to a fair trial for all individuals, however heinous their crimes may be, will be a moral loss against those who preach hatred and violence.

From our recent experience, we have learnt that terrorist attacks against innocent and unsuspecting civilians threaten the preservation of the rule of law as well as human rights; and terrorism can broadly be identified with the use of violent methods in place of the ordinary tools of civic engagement and political participation. It has become an increasingly recurrent strategy for insurgent movements as well as identity-based groups to make their voice heard through armed attacks and bomb blasts in place of public dialogue. Independent India is no stranger to the problem of tackling armed terrorists and has faced long-running

---

*This is based on Chief Justice of India K.G. Balakrishnan's presidential address at the inaugural session of the international conference of jurists on 'Terrorism, Rule of Law & Human Rights' in New Delhi on 13 December 2008.

insurgencies as well as sporadic attacks in many parts of the country.

However, in the age of easy international travel and advanced communications, terrorist networks have also assumed cross-border dimensions. In many instances, attacks are planned by individuals located in different countries who use modern technology to collaborate for the transfer of funds and procurement of advanced weapons. This clearly means that terrorism is an international problem and requires effective multilateral engagement between various nations.

A Challenge

For the international legal community, this poses a doctrinal as well as practical challenge. I say this because from the prism of international legal norms, prescriptions against violent attacks have traditionally evolved under two categories—first, those related to armed conflict between nations, and second, those pertaining to internal disturbances within a nation. While the conduct and consequences of armed conflicts between nations—such as wars and border skirmishes—are regulated by international criminal law and humanitarian law, the occurrence of internal disturbances within a nation are largely considered to be the subject-matter of that particular nation's domestic criminal justice system and constitutional principles.

It is often perceived that these doctrinal demarcations actually inhibit international cooperation for cracking down on terrorist cells with cross-border networks. In the absence of bilateral treaties for extradition or assistance in investigation, there is no clear legal basis for international cooperation in investigating terrorist attacks—which are usually classified as internal disturbances in the nation where they took place. Since there are no clear and consistent norms to guide collaboration between nations in acting against terrorists, countries like the United States have invented their own doctrines such as 'pre-emptive action' to justify counter-terrorism operations in foreign nations.

However, the pursuit of terrorists alone cannot be a justification for arbitrarily breaching another nation's sovereignty. In this scenario, one strategy that has been suggested is that of recognizing terrorist attacks as coming within a new 'hybrid' category of armed conflict, wherein obligations can be placed on different countries to collaborate in the investigation and prosecution of terrorist attacks that have taken place in a particular country. This calls for a blurring of the distinction between the international and domestic nature of armed conflict when it comes to terrorist strikes.

Another suggestion that has been made in this regard is that of treating terrorist attacks as offences recognized under International Criminal Law, such as 'crimes against humanity', which can then be tried before a supranational tribunal such as the International Criminal Court (ICC). However, the obvious practical problem with this suggestion is that prosecutions before this court need to be initiated by the United Nations Security Council (UNSC) and the latter body may be reluctant to do so in instances of one-off terrorist attacks as opposed to continuing conflicts.

Practical Constraint

Yet another practical constraint that has been brought to the fore with the Mumbai attacks has been the question of holding governments responsible for the actions of non-state actors. While one can say that there is a moral duty on all governments to prevent and restrain the activities of militant groups on their soil, this is easier said than done. For example, several terrorist groups are able to organize financial support and procure weapons even in Western nations where the policing and criminal justice systems are perceived to be relatively stronger than in the subcontinent.

Coming to the domestic setting, I must state that the symbolic impact of terrorist attacks on the minds of ordinary citizens has also been considerably amplified by the role of pervasive media coverage. In India, the proliferation of 24-hour television news channels and the digital medium has ensured that quite often some disturbing images and statements reach a very wide audience. One of the ill-effects of unrestrained coverage is that of provoking anger among the masses. While it is fair for the media to prompt public criticism of inadequacies in the security and law-enforcement apparatus, there is also a possibility of such resentment turning into an irrational desire for retribution.

Furthermore, the trauma resulting from the terrorist attacks may be used as a justification for undue curtailment of individual rights and liberties. Instead of offering a considered response to the growth of terrorism, a country may resort to questionable methods such as permitting indefinite detention of terror suspects, the use of coercive interrogation techniques, and the denial of the right to fair trial. Outside the criminal justice system, the fear generated by terrorist attacks may also be linked to increasing governmental surveillance over citizens and unfair restrictions on immigration.

'Slippery Slope'

In recent years, the most prominent example of this 'slippery slope' for the curtailment of individual rights is the treatment of the detainees in Guantanamo Bay who were arrested by US authorities in the wake of the 9/11 attacks. It is alleged that they have detained hundreds of suspects for long periods, often without the filing of charges or access to independent judicial remedies.

For its part the US administration has defended these practices by asserting that the detainees at Guantanamo Bay have safeguards such as appeals before military commissions, administrative review boards and combatant status review tribunals. A follow up to this in *Hamdan v. Rumsfeld* (126 S. Ct. 2749 [2006]) led to the ruling that the terror suspects could not be denied the right of habeas corpus and should be granted access to civilian courts. The rationale for this was that the various military tribunals did not possess the requisite degree of independence to try suspects who had been apprehended and detained by the military authorities themselves.

Even in the United Kingdom, the House of Lords in the *Belmarsh* decision (*A v. Secretary of State for the Home Department*, [2004] UKHL 56) ruled against a provision in the Anti-Terrorism, Crime and Security Act, 2001, which allowed the indefinite detention of foreign terror suspects. This ruling prompted the enactment of the Prevention of Terrorism Act, 2005, which was fiercely debated. The British Parliament accepted a 42-day period as the maximum permissible for detention without charges, subject to judicial checks. Evidently, the judiciary in these two countries has played a moderating role in checking the excesses that have crept into the response against terrorism.

In some circles, it is argued that the judiciary places unnecessary curbs on the power of the investigating agencies to tackle terrorism. In India, those who subscribe to this view also demand changes in our criminal and evidence law—such as provisions for longer periods of preventive detention and confessions made before police officials to be made admissible in court. While the ultimate choice in this regard lies with the legislature, we must be careful not to trample upon constitutional principles such as 'substantive due process'. This guarantee was read into the conception of 'personal liberty' under Article 21 of the Constitution of India by our Supreme Court. (This idea of 'substantive due process' was incorporated through the decision in *Maneka Gandhi v. Union of India*, AIR 1978 SC 597.) The necessary implication of this is that all governmental action, even in exceptional times, must meet the standards of reasonableness, non-arbitrariness and non-discrimination.

This implies that we must be wary of the use of torture and other forms of coercive interrogation techniques by law enforcement agencies. Coercive interrogation techniques mostly induce false confessions and do not help in preventing terrorist attacks. Furthermore, the tolerance of the same can breed a sense of complacency if they are viewed as an easy way out by investigative agencies.

Need for Professionalism

The apprehension and interrogation of terror suspects must also be done in a thoroughly professional manner, with the provision of adequate judicial scrutiny as mandated in the Code of Criminal Procedure. This is required because in recent counter-terrorist operations, there have been several reports of arbitrary arrests of individuals belonging to certain communities and the concoction of evidence—such as the production of similarly worded confession statements by detained suspects in different places. The proposal for the admissibility of confessional statements made before the police is also problematic since there are fears that such a change will incentivize torture and coercive interrogation by investigative agencies in order to seek convictions rather than engaging in thorough investigation.

The role of the judiciary in this regard should not be misunderstood. Adherence to the constitutional principle of 'substantive due process' is an essential part of our collective response to terrorism. As part of the legal community, we must uphold the right to fair trial for all individuals, irrespective of how heinous their crimes may be. If we accept a dilution of this right, it will count as a moral loss against those who preach hatred and violence. We must not confuse between what distinguishes the deliberations of a mature democratic society from the misguided actions of a few.

13

Acts of Terror and Terrorizing Act: Unfolding Indian Tragedy*

SUKLA SEN

In some circles, it is argued that the judiciary places unnecessary curbs on the power of the investigating agencies to tackle terrorism. In India, those who subscribe to this view also demand changes in our criminal and evidence law—such as provisions for longer periods of preventive detention and confessions made before police officials to be made admissible in court. While the ultimate choice in this regard lies with the legislature, we must be careful not to trample upon constitutional principles such as 'substantive due process'.

...

The role of the judiciary in this regard should not be misunderstood. Adherence to the constitutional principle of 'substantive due process' is an essential part of our collective response to terrorism. As part of the legal community, we must uphold the right to fair trial for all individuals, irrespective of how heinous their crimes may be. If we accept a dilution of this right, it will count as a moral loss against those who preach hatred and violence.

K.G. Balakrishnan, Chief Justice of India[1]

*The article is already published in South Asia Citizens Web on 19 December 2008 and is available online at www.sacw.net

It is a matter of great shame and concern that the amended UAPA Act which had been placed before the Lok Sabha on Tuesday evening was passed unanimously the very next day, on 17 December.

Similarly, the Rajya Sabha passed it the following evening.

This is almost a rerun of the shameful saga of hurried passage of the highly controversial and contested SEZ Act in early 2005. There is, however, at least one crucial difference. In the earlier case, it was a rather quiet affair, almost a hush-hush. This time it was done amidst ugly chest-thumping. Last time, in the Lok Sabha, the BJP did not even participate in the deliberations. This time they claimed with full gusto the credit (sic) for the passage of the Bill overshadowing its official sponsors.

While the full details remain to be accessed and analyzed it is pretty much clear that most of the provisions of the earlier scrapped POTA—scrapped on account of strong reactions triggered by a history of huge misuse against the minorities, other marginalized sections of the society, people struggling against social and political injustices and also known opponents of those in positions of power—have been brought back. Only the provision for legal admissibility of a 'confession' made in police custody is left out. But there are other areas, where its reach has further extended. The most important aspect, however, is that the court has to treat an accused as guilty till proved otherwise and unless the court finds the accused prima facie innocent it won't grant any bail to the accused. In case of a 'foreign national', there is just no provision for any bail, whatever. This evidently runs counter to the recent Supreme Court directive that during a trial granting of bail should be the norm, and rejection an exception.

Even the BJP's star speaker in the Rajya Sabha, Arun Jaitley, had to thus admit in course of his shrill advocacy for a draconian Act while supporting the Bill:

It is obvious that an anti terror law is not a substitute for stronger intelligence and security responses. You need a powerful intelligence mechanism which infiltrates into the enemy camp and brings you advance information of what the enemy is planning. The intelligence has to be coordinated and then effectively passed on to those who will take preventive measures. Your security responses have to be fast. Your commando reactions must send fear into the enemy mind. Obviously, an anti terror law is not a replacement of all these.

(Arun Jaitley speech in Rajya Sabha)[2]

It is not necessary here to get into the utterly perverse nature of Jaitley's foundational assumption of some perpetual enmity and a permanent 'enemy camp' except for noting that this is the central element of mobilization strategy of the Hindutva Brigade in pursuance of its 'Hindu Rashtra' project—ideological negation and physical liquidation of 'secular democratic' India. But what is more relevant is that even he cannot run away from the obvious fact that draconian laws are no substitute for good intelligence gathering (to prevent acts of terrorism) and prompt and effective response to such acts when they take place nevertheless.

A rider, a forewarning, issued by the incumbent Chief Justice of India, in a recent article of his is extremely instructive in the current context:

> [T]he trauma resulting from the terrorist attacks may be used as a justification for undue curtailment of individual rights and liberties. Instead of offering a considered response to the growth of terrorism, a country may resort to questionable methods such as permitting indefinite detention of terror suspects, the use of coercive interrogation techniques, and the denial of the right to fair trial. Outside the criminal justice system, the fear generated by terrorist attacks may also be linked to increasing governmental surveillance over citizens and unfair restrictions on immigration.
>
> ...
>
> This implies that we must be wary of the use of torture and other forms of coercive interrogation techniques by law enforcement agencies. Coercive interrogation techniques mostly induce false confessions and do not help in preventing terrorist attacks. Furthermore, the tolerance of the same can breed a sense of complacency if they are viewed as an easy way out by investigative agencies.
>
> (K.G. Balakrishnan)[3]

Pretty unfortunately, but rather expectedly, the entire thrust of the discourse spearheaded by the outraged elite is to 'tighten the law' to ensure 'conviction' of the accused by granting more powers to the law enforcing agencies whose performance in stalling terrorist attacks amidst repeated claims of busting the 'terror modules' and capturing, and also 'neutralizing' through encounters, the (innumerable) 'masterminds' remains utterly and increasingly dismal. Highly conspicuous is any anxiety to ensure an efficient investigation and effective intelligence gathering and making those responsible for failures accountable for their failures.

Draconian laws, let there be no confusion, will only tend to turn the high-handed, corrupt and lousy police force even more so and thereby further worsen the situation. Not that there will not be more convictions and many more arrests, indefinite detentions, custodial and encounter deaths. The continued incarceration of Dr Binayak Sen—a dedicated doctor of highest distinction and a human rights activist of national stature—behind the bars since May 2007 on apparently trumped up charges despite national and global protests, even without the aid of the newly brushed up UAPA Act, is enough of a pointer. But that will not stop or deter terrorism, rather further aggravate. It is a great tragedy that such measure is being sold and consumed considered as the silver bullet in spite of clearly proven track record of gross failures. The attack on the Indian Parliament, the Red Fort, Akshardham Temple in Gandhinagar and also the hijacking of an Indian Airlines plane to Kandahar are just a few examples. All these are, incidentally, of somewhat similar nature as that of the latest attack in Mumbai.

The latest terror attack in Mumbai, which is somewhat atypical in the context of endless terror attacks in India since the one on 12 March 1993—flowing directly from the preceding bloodbath sparked on 6 January 1993—has, however, one common characteristic. That is the gross failure of intelligence. Intelligence gathering and sorting out of the same through interactions of various agencies into actionable knowledge has various stages and levels. The gathering itself has essentially two categories—domestic and external. The external element is of course the charge of a very specialized agency mainly through a set of trained 'spies', and tips from other 'friendly' agencies. The internal gathering process is, however, far more varied. Even then the base, the most crucial element, is constituted of intelligence gathering at the grassroots level. Here the present practice is to obtain information through paid 'informers'—all sorts of shady characters, petty and professional criminals. Given the extremely negative image of the police vis-à-vis the local communities, it could hardly be otherwise. But this method cannot but be far less efficient than it would have been in case of voluntary and free flow of information from the common citizenry. But that would call for a very different image of the police, a very different relationship with the local communities. Instead of an institution symbolizing an embodiment of torture and oppression, the police need to have a people-friendly image in order to make that possible. But in such an event, not only intelligence gathering would be far more efficient—that would rather be a fringe benefit—the maintenance of 'law and order' itself would be much smoother.

Nothing can be truer and more forthright than a recent assessment of the current state of Indian policing as contained in a statement issued by the Asian

Human Rights Commission on the last 2 December, in the wake of the terror attack in Mumbai.

The fact remains that the Maharashtra State Police, like any other state police force in the country, can hardly do anything to avert these incidents. The state of policing in the country is in such demise that it has completely severed its contact with the people. Most police officers contact the members of the public only to demand bribes. Corruption in the police service is at such levels that even in order to lodge a complaint the complainant has to pay a bribe. Police brutality is so rampant in the country that the sight of a police uniform is enough to scare an ordinary person, particularly among the poor population. Information, independent of its nature, has to be forced out of the ordinary people. Information obtained under the threat of violence is tainted and cannot be acted upon. Terrorists are different from the ordinary people in the sense that they have money, better training and equipment at their disposal to achieve their goals. They can bribe the police and are in fact doing so.

...

To expect an ordinary Indian to approach the local police with information is an impossibility in the country. An example is the statements made by the parents who lost their children in the infamous 2006 December Noida serial murder case. The case began [only] after the recovery of the skeletal remains of missing children in Nithari village in the outskirts of Noida city close to New Delhi.

(Asian Human Rights Commission, 2008)[4]

The unfortunate 'unanimous' passage of the freshly amended Unlawful Activities (Prevention) Act is only an indicator of the deep rot in the system. It is no less revealing that during the debates no one reportedly raised the very sensible and in fact obvious demand for a credible public enquiry covering all the aspects of widely alleged intelligence failure, response lags and lapses, who are behind the attack—to work out a set of thoughtful and rational responses to make the system at least somewhat less vulnerable the next time round; to make the reoccurrence significantly less probable; to make such a tragedy far less costly if it manages to happen nevertheless. We had only chest thumping demagoguery, clamour for draconian laws and war cries all around.

Instead of helping contain terrorism, let alone eradicating, it will only further aggravate social tensions through legitimization of corrupt high-handedness of the police force and targeting of specific segments of the society with full protections of the law. It was perhaps Gorky who had pronounced that if order is injustice then disorder is the beginning of justice. Unfortunately, law itself predictably turning more and more unlawful and tyrannical, more and more youngsters would tend to embrace that as a piece of divine wisdom with disastrous consequences on all sides to follow.

That even the sage words of the serving Chief Justice of India stand so casually dismissed only goes to further underscore the depth of the tragedy we have dug ourselves in.

Only an awakened common citizenry refusing to succumb to the easy lure of ugly blood lust triggered by such disasters as the last terror attack in Mumbai and steadfastly demanding thoughtful actions and radical reforms to prevent recurrence of such shameful failure is the way to get ourselves out.

Notes

1. Balakrishnan, K.G. 2008. 'Terrorism, Rule of Law and Human Rights'. Available online at http://www.hindu.com/2008/12/16/stories/2008121653310800.htm, accesed on 19 December 2008.
2. Arun Jaitley's speech in Rajya Sabha on NIA, UAPA Bills on 18 December 2008. Available online at http://offstumped.nationalinterest.in/2008/12/18/arun-jaitleys-speech-in-rajya-sabha-on-nia-uapa-bills, accessed on 19 Decemer 2008.
3. Balakrishnan, K.G. 2008. 'Terrorism, Rule of law, and Human Rights'. Available online at http://www.hindu.com/2008/12/16/stories/2008121653310800.htm, accessed on 19 December 2008.
4. Asian Human Rights Commission. '"Super Cop" is no Solution to Terrorist Threat'. Available online at http://www.ahrchk.net/statements/mainfile.php/2008statements/1789/, accessed on 19 December 2008.

14

Our Politicians are Still not Listening*

COLIN GONSALVES

One would have thought that after the Bombay attack and the public outpouring of resentment against politicians, that the establishment would get its act in order. One would expect that careful thought would go into the making of proposals to combat terrorism and to keep the people secure. Instead what do we find? The same old clichés and the usual attack on human rights activists.

What the people of India expected was that the governments would give careful thought to making the police a professional fighting force oriented towards the security of the ordinary citizens of India rather than operating, as it does now, as the protectors of politicians. They also expected that the police would eliminate from its ranks the use of torture and the vice of corruption, two aspects of policing today that make the general public both distrustful and fearful of the police.

Listening carefully, however, to the statements of BJP and Congress politicians in the media, one

*The article has already been published in *Mail Today* on 20 December 2008.

can find no reference to the demands of the people. Politicians are obviously distracted by the national elections scheduled for early next year and even such a serious incident of terrorism as the Bombay attack figures even now in their consciousness as a vote catching exercise.

In a knee-jerk reaction, GOI proposes to enact The Unlawful Activities (Prevention) Amendment Act, 2008. Under Section 15, the prosecution is to be granted up to 180 days to file a chargesheet (it is a 90-day limit today after which the accused is granted bail mandatorily), the provisions for bail are stricter, and if arms or explosives are proved to be recovered from the accused, then the court is entitled to presume that the accused has committed a terrorist act.

Indian criminal law provisions rank among the strictest in the world. In the US and the UK, even after the terrorist attacks in those countries, the maximum period of detention without a chargesheet is 2 days and 28 days, respectively. The provisions in India for search and seizures are the most liberal in the world.

Supreme Court decisions to the effect that even if the searches and seizures are illegal they may still be relied upon in evidence against the accused, has given the police a free hand to do all kinds of hanky panky while conducting raids. Amendments have been made in various statutes to permit interceptions of communications.

Supreme Court decisions after 2000 have watered down the criminal law protection of accused persons and have lowered the criminal law standard of proof beyond reasonable doubt to such an extent that international jurists are appalled by the way in which the Indian courts are convicting accused persons. Why then, with such strict laws and with such a convicting judiciary, did the Bombay attack happen with such impunity? The answer is simple. The problem in India lies not in the law but in its implementation.

This is where the main demands of the people that the police become a professional force, that law and order be separated from the investigation of crimes, and that corruption and violence be eliminated, becomes important. The central government also proposes to pass The National Investigation Agency Bill, 2008 which will see the setting up of a national body to oversee the investigation and prosecution of terrorist offences. Here again the approach is cosmetic rather than substantial and the aim is to impress rather than protect. The Central Bureau of Investigation (CBI) is today a national body for the investigation of all serious crimes. The only difference between the CBI and the NIA is that the former is required to take the permission of the states prior to acting within the state, whereas the NIA can operate without consent. But if all the states are agreed, as indeed they are, that terrorism ought to be fought at the national level as well, then there ought to be no difficulty for the central government to consult the legislatures of the states in a transparent manner, to obtain consent for the CBI to operate throughout the country.

All that would be necessary thereafter is for the central government to administratively upgrade the CBI.

Though it must be said to the credit of the Union Government that they have not succumbed to the temptation to introduce the draconian POTA provision authorizing confessions to a police officer (which rendered POTA trials farcical), the reference to Left wing Extremism in the Statements of Objects and Reasons is disappointing.

Naxalism has deep social roots in injustice, poverty and state violence, unlike the senseless terrorism of Pakistani agents. Like the IRA in Ireland, it must be recognized as a political tendency and negotiated with politically. The reasons for the growth of naxalism must be understood as requiring a radical shift from the inequities of globalization to a more socialistic programme where the common person is treated with dignity. In the present political situation, however, one can only see hysteria and the lack of reason.

15
Terrorism: Are Stronger Laws the Answer?*

PRASHANT BHUSHAN

The terrorist attack on two five star hotels in Mumbai has led to a lot of jingoism and muscle-flexing in the media, and on the streets. 'Enough is enough', 'we will not pay our taxes' and 'we must destroy terrorist training camps in Pakistan' are the kind of cries that are heard most frequently. 'Get tough on terror' is the new mantra and among other things, getting tough means bringing tougher laws. The UPA government, which repealed POTA just four years ago because it was found to be draconian, misused and counter-productive, has now used the jingoism to enact a 'tougher terror law' in the form of amendments in the already draconian Unlawful Activities Prevention Act. These amendments were introduced in Parliament on the 15 December and passed the next day with virtually no debate and without any opportunity to civil society to study, digest and debate the implications of the amendments.

Those who have been clamouring for tougher laws often do not know what makes the law tough, and

---

*The article has already been published in *The Hindu*, January 2009.

how 'tougher' laws would deter or prevent terrorism. In the first place, it must be understood that a law can only help to keep in custody and prosecute and convict any person who has been arrested. No law, however tough or draconian, can deter or deal with suicidal terrorists who are willing to die before they are caught. The prospect of no bail or the prospect of being convicted is hardly likely to scare or deter the kind of terrorists who attacked Mumbai. In fact, in Iraq, the security forces or the Army can detain or keep in detention indefinitely or even shoot down any person at will. The police or security forces cannot have more draconian powers than that. Yet, those powers, far from bringing down terrorism in Iraq, have only led to conditions which have created more terrorists who are blowing up themselves and hundreds of people every day.

When POTA was repealed, some of its draconian provisions had been engrafted into the Unlawful Activities (Prevention) Act. Those, along with The Chhattisgarh Public Security Act, whose provisions make it an offence to provide any kind of assistance to a banned organization or a person belonging to a banned organization, have been used to incarcerate Binayak Sen, the General Secretary of the PUCL. Sen, unquestionably one of the most selfless activists, spent a good part of his life in setting up public health clinics in remote areas of Chhattisgarh. He has been in detention for the last one and half years on the charge that he has 'assisted' Maoists who were in jail by taking letters from them and giving them to their comrades. It matters not that these letters he is alleged to have carried did not contain anything subversive. The mere fact that he is alleged to have carried letters from an alleged Maoist is enough to charge him with 'assisting' an unlawful (Maoist) organization and thus a terrorist act.

Denial of bail under POTA had only allowed the investigative agencies to keep under detention innocent persons, against whom the investigative agencies had no evidence of terrorism. No court would grant bail anyway to a person against whom there is any evidence of involvement in any terrorist act. No government has ever come up with a case that some terrorist act was committed by a person who was arrested earlier but released on bail because of the absence of 'stronger laws'. Similarly, everybody knows that police confessions can be obtained from anyone by torture or under the threat of torture. They are a totally unsafe and unreliable basis for charging or convicting any person. These draconian provisions of POTA and its predecessor TADA had only encouraged the police to detain innocent persons indefinitely, chargesheet them on the basis of police confessions and then prosecute them in trials which go on for years. Once having arrested the persons and chargesheeted them, the police claim that the case has been solved. During this time, these persons are usually tortured in custody, and forced to confess. Their prolonged incarcerations lead to the permanent loss of their reputation and the economic destruction of their families. The fact that most of the persons chargesheeted under these draconian laws were innocent is clear from the fact that more than 98 per cent of them were eventually acquitted. But their acquittal came only after an enormous toll on their reputation, health, lives and the economic survival of their families. This has not only caused great injustice to thousands of innocent persons who have been unfairly arrested and victimized by the investigative agencies in this manner, it is one of the major causes of the insecurity, alienation and anger of the minorities against the police, the criminal justice system and indeed the ruling establishment of the country.

This is indeed the finding of several People's Tribunals which have extensively heard the testimonies of large numbers of persons who were victimized by these Acts. The People's Tribunal on POTA, consisting of eminent jurists like Ram Jethmalani, Justice Suresh, Justice D.K. Basu, K.G. Kannabiran and other eminent persons opined in their report in 2004 that 'our review of victim and expert testimony shows that the misuse of the Act is inseperable from its normal use. It is a Statute meant to terrorise, not so much the terrorists as ordinary civilians—particularly the poor and disadvantaged such as dalits, religious minorities, adivasis and working people (Interim Observation by Peoples' Tribunal).'

A People's Tribunal on the terror investigations of the police in various states of the country was held in Hyderabad in August 2008. The jury consisted of two former Chief Justices, several other eminent academics, lawyers and social scientists. They came to the unanimous conclusion that:

The testimonies showed that a large number of innocent young Muslims have been and are being victimized by the police on the charge of being involved in various terrorist acts across the country. This is particularly so in Maharashtra, Gujarat, Madhya Pradesh, Andhra Pradesh and Rajasthan, though not limited to these States.

This victimization and demonization of Muslims in the guise of investigation of terror offences, is having a very serious psychological impact on the minds of not only the families of the victims but also other members of the community. It is leading to a very strong sense of insecurity and alienation which may lead to frightful consequences for the nation.

The amendments now rushed through in the Unlawful Activities Act undoubtedly make it more draconian by giving more powers to the police to search, arrest, keep in police custody and in jail persons on mere subjective suspicion even if they have no evidence of their being involved in any terrorist Acts. The newly introduced Section 43A of the act empowers an officer of a designated authority to search any premises or arrest any person of whom he has 'reason to believe or knows' that he has a 'design to commit an offence under the Act'.

Further, police officers investigating an offence under the Act have (with the approval of the SP) been empowered to require any organization or any individual to furnish any information that the officer may demand for his investigation. The failure to furnish such information has been made punishable with up to three years imprisonment. Such a provision can and will easily be misused by the police to harass all kinds of activists, lawyers, doctors and journalists who stand up for, or provide any assistance, even legal or medical, to an alleged terrorist.

The maximum period for keeping persons in police custody has been extended from 15 to 30 days. Police custody is sought for 'custodial interrogation' which we all know is a euphemism for custodial torture. India has the highest number of custodial deaths in the world and is among the few countries which have not signed the UN convention on torture. Though the Constitution provides that no one can be compelled to be a witness against himself, yet such coercive 'custodial interrogation' is being allowed by the courts for months without end. Abu Basheer, the Azamgarh cleric who has been dubbed as one of the many 'Masterminds' of the serial blasts in Ahmedabad, Jaipur and Delhi, has been continuously kept in police custody for more than 6 months now by arresting him serially (after every 15 days) in one after another of the more than 25 FIRs that have been registered in Ahmedabad, Jaipur and Delhi for the serial blasts.

The Code of Criminal Procedure provides that if the chargesheet against an arrested person is not filed within 90 days, he will be entitled to bail. This is for the reason, that till the chargesheet is filed, it is virtually impossible for an arrested person to get bail, even if the police have no evidence against him. The new amendments also extend the maximum period for filing a chargesheet against an arrestee to 180 days. Another amendment makes bail virtually impossible even during trial. It provides that an 'accused person shall not be released on bail or on his own bond, if the court on a perusal of the case diary or the report made under section 173 (the chargesheet) of the code is of the opinion that there are reasonable grounds for believing that the accusations against the persons are prima facie true'.

These amendments make the Unlawful Activities Act as or more draconian than POTA. The only draconian provision of POTA left out in this Act now is the admissibility of police confessions.

Far from curbing terror, we find that draconian laws, used by a corrupt and communal police, are creating conditions which will only exacerbate the problem. The normal laws of the land are adequate to deal with terror offences. The problem lies with the police, which is the implementing agency. The Supreme Court had issued many directions in September 2006 to implement police reforms which several expert agencies of the government had recommended many years ago, but which had not been implemented. They included, setting up independent State and National Security Commissions, Police Establishment Boards, Police Complaints Authorities and giving a minimum tenure to heads of field police officers at all levels including Police Chiefs. The thrust of these recommendations was to make the police and investigative agencies accountable to the law and free them from the strangulating control of the political executive. Neither the central nor most of the state governments have implemented the directions of the Supreme Court about the police reforms. None of the major political parties are prepared to relinquish their political control over the police.

Implementation of reforms within the police and intelligence agencies should certainly improve security and reduce terror attacks. But that will not eliminate the problem. Israel, with the most efficient intelligence, security and police has not been able to eliminate the problem, despite the small size of the country. They have suicide attacks almost every month. No amount of intelligence or security can stop terrorists who are willing to give up their lives. They can only be stopped if their motivation is eliminated. That will require what Chomsky advised in the wake of 9/11. He said, 'As to how to react (to 9/11), we have a choice. We can express justified horror; we can seek to understand what may have led to the crimes, which means making an effort to enter into the minds of the likely perpetrators.... We may try to understand, or refuse to do so, contributing to the likelihood that much worse lies ahead' (Chomsky).

Eventually, understanding the motivations of the terrorists and dealing with the injustices that pervade our society, and repairing the institutions of justice, particularly the police and the judiciary, will be a much more effective way of fighting terror, than laws which give more draconian powers to corrupt and insensitive police organizations.

References

Chomsky, Noam. 2001. *A Quick Reaction*. CounterPunch.

People's Tribunal on the Atrocities Committed Against Minorities in the Name of Fighting Terrorism, 22–24 August 2008, Hyderabad. Organized by ANHAD, HRLN and PEACE. Available online at http://www.anhadin.net/article44.html, accessed on 26 August 2008.

16
Lessons from the Mumbai Attack*

GAUTAM NAVLAKHA

More than three months after the Mumbai attack, focus remains on Islamabad's dilatory tactics and frustration at getting the Pakistan government to cooperate in investigating the possible links and support network of the armed gunmen. It is granted that the audacious commando-style operation, attacking several places simultaneously, represents a paradigm shift in the conduct of low-intensity urban warfare. The planning, training, financing and logistics involved suggest that swathes of Pakistani territory have become captive of non-state actors who operate virtually at will, with or without the connivance of the Pakistani authorities. Although multiple centres of power, jostling for pre-eminence, are said to be a complicating factor, there appears to be consensus among the various power centres to drag the investigation, turning it into an Indo-Pak problem and using it to gain some leeway in negotiations with the US in the war against the Taliban and Al Qaeda on its western frontier, unmindful of its impact on relations with India or on its own society. The Pakistani military has claimed that it cannot spare

*This article has been published earlier in *Economic and Political Weekly*, Vol. 44, No. 11, 14–20 March 2009.

forces to restore the state's authority in the Swat region because of tensions with India on its eastern borders. This is a high risk policy to link tensions with India to allow the Taliban to consolidate itself in the Swat region and to use the Mumbai attack investigations to extract some gains vis-à-vis India.

Since war as an option was ruled out by New Delhi,[1] and it lacks leverage over Islamabad, few options are available to the Indian government. Options have further narrowed by the latter choosing to put pressure on Pakistani civil society by obstructing people-to-people contacts. This is compounded by competitive jingoism between the Bharatiya Janata Party (BJP) and the Congress over Pakistan and terrorism as the country nears its 15th parliamentary elections. In this sense, the current stand-off has raised the stakes for both India and Pakistan and, with or without another attack, can precipitate matters towards a free fight. Independent of what Pakistan does, or chooses not to do, obsessive concern has its negative fallout. By projecting that Pakistan is the source of our troubles it is implied that, but for Pakistan's support for terrorism, things would be hunky-dory, or that without Pakistan's cooperation, the Indian state is helpless to prevent terror attacks. Such an approach diverts attention from looking at where the Indian state has gone wrong, empowers chauvinists, and enables the authorities to favour harsh laws and augment military resources, without too many questions being asked.[2] In other words, as the Pakistani people grapple with their establishment, we in India need to focus on ours.

Preparedness or Augmentation

To believe that the security apparatus will perform better when it is armed with harsh laws and, simultaneously, scarce resources are diverted to buy modern weapons and augment manpower, is a colossal misrepresentation of facts. By abbreviating constitutional freedoms or recruiting more security personnel, and freeing them from accountability, it is not possible to prevent mass murders. Consider the following facts. The attack by armed gunmen on 26 November last year could have been prevented by the Indian navy, the coast guard and the Mumbai police with the existing resources at their command, failing which, had not security been lowered at the hotels, due to misappraisal by the state police, the gunmen could have met some resistance, and their entry could have been delayed. Even if all this had failed, the 58-hour long stand-off could have been cut short, if commandos had not arrived 12 hours later, due to unavailability of a plane at Delhi to ferry the commandos, or if they did not have to wait, for more than an hour at the Mumbai airport, for a bus to take them to the scene of the crime. Commando operations could have been made relatively easier, if they had access to maps/drawings of the buildings, which further complicated the operations. All this did not require extraordinary laws or sophisticated weaponry, but preparedness, since India has been insisting that it has been subjected to terrorism since the 1980s. Surely three decades is long enough to get our act together.

For instance, a lot has been written about the need for sophisticated weaponry and commando-style training for the police force. But little focus has been placed on something as basic as vacant posts of 113,779 constables in the police force across the country. Constables are the backbone of beat policing, important for law and order and for gathering human intelligence. However, there has been an inbuilt bias in favour of armed police at the expense of civil police.[3] Therefore, filling these vacancies is one thing. But to use the Mumbai attack to justify raising 125 additional battalions of central paramilitary formations, that is recruitment of 1.4 lakh personnel over the next two to three years, including four battalions for National Security Guards (NSG) commandos, or massive purchase of weapons is, quite simply, 'barking up the wrong tree'.[4] An NSG commando force of 7,500 personnel is not a small force. But 1,700 commandos, or one-fourth of the strength, are engaged in static VIP duty. The presence of four more NSG battalions will not, by itself, bring about a quick response.[5] After all, on 24 December 1999, during the hijacking of IC-814, the NSG commandos could not reach Amritsar airport on time because, reportedly, they were caught in a traffic jam! In 2008, in Mumbai, the problem was non-availability of transportation. In both cases it was the lethargic response or unpreparedness of the administration which lay behind the delay.

Yet, we are expected to believe that we are short of security personnel and of military hardware despite having spent, between 2001–02 and 2006–07, no less than Rs 2,780,491 crore on military augmentation.[6]

It is also argued that police force must be armed with automatic weapons and that .303 rifles are outdated. This is open to question because armed police formations and individual armed gunmen cannot be compared. Regular training of police personnel and quick issuance of weapons from armoury during crisis cannot be substituted by purchasing lethal weapons. Besides, issuing police force kalashnikovs can cause greater harm than good in crowded urban locations. Furthermore, such commando-style encounters are not the norm when mass murderers have used a range of materials, from kalashnikovs, bombs, swords, trishuls, lathis, pen knives, etc. It is also worth noting that it was .303 carrying and baton-wielding Mumbai constables who managed to overpower Ajmal Kasab, thereby enabling Mumbai crime branch sleuths to put together a credible case.

Are Harsh Laws the Answer?

Take the next argument—that 'terrorism' is a crime which requires moving away from normal criminal legal provisions and diluting due process. But 'terrorists' do not belong to a different species, which can be singled out. It is also a known fact that by relaxing procedures and lowering the threshold for collection of evidence, an innocent can get implicated and the real culprit escape justice. There are few occasions when a person is arrested red-handed from the scene of the crime. In most cases, people are picked up as 'suspects' and investigators then try to establish their connection with the crime. The case of Irshad Ali (*The Times of India*, 13 September 2007) also shows that despite the Central Bureau of Investigation (CBI) exonerating him and indicting the Special Cell of the Delhi Police for preparing a false case with fake recovery of RDX, the victim continues to languish in jail and the Special Cell refuses to admit its wrongdoing. Verily, the wheels of justice grind painfully slow even when they begin to roll. Indeed, the CBI officer who investigated this case on the Delhi High Court's direction recently complained that he was being threatened by personnel of the Special Cell! This being the state of affairs in the capital city of Delhi, then, when the law turns liberal jurisprudence on its head, as the new set of amendments to Unlawful Activities Prevention Act (especially Section 43) does, by placing the onus of proving innocence on the accused, because his/her fingerprints were found at the scene of the crime or that weapons were recovered from him/her, then it ignores the reality that it is perfectly possible in India to plant evidence or foist false cases against someone by virtue of the fact that the person is Muslim, dalit, adivasi or Naxalite.

Conversely, police, prosecutors and the lower judiciary provide greater latitude to suspected mass murderers who are Hindus, as is evident from the recent case of Gujarat minister Maya Kodnani and Vishwa Hindu Parishad leader Jayant Patel who evaded summons issued by the Supreme Court-appointed Special Investigation Team and managed to get anticipatory bail despite being implicated in the Naroda Patiya mass murder. It is worth noting that the Godhra accused have yet to get bail despite the Prevention of Terrorism Act (POTA) being revoked against them. In other words, we cannot be blind to the fact that, in India, draconian laws, such as the Unlawful Activities Prevention Act (UAPA), POTA, Terrorist and Disruptive Activities (Prevention) Act (TADA) or Chapter VI of the Indian Penal Code (IPC) on offences against the state have been used, selectively and deliberately, to target ethnic communities and the underclass. Besides, when the law defines unlawful acts and terrorism vaguely or when it proscribes political ideologies, thereby turning criminal what is otherwise legitimate, then the law becomes intrinsically unjust and ends up causing great harm, as Binayak Sen and Arun Ferreira's cases so well illustrate. Finally, the fact that such laws exclude state agencies from its purview, assuming that they cannot be guilty of carrying out acts of mass murder or of conniving in such acts carried out by non-state actors, because they are said to be acting in 'good faith', it ends up subverting the criminal justice system. The truth is that discrimination and persecution beget resentment and nurture a sense of revenge.

Therefore, we need to remind ourselves that the Pakistani state is not unique insofar as its patronage of 'majoritarian' communal-fascist groups is concerned. Or else how diligent and fair has the Indian state been in going after mass murderers when they have single-mindedly focused on Muslims as suspects behind almost all such incidents, prior to the Malegaon bomb blast in 2008? What stopped the investigating and intelligence agencies from even entertaining the likely involvement of Hindu fascists in bomb blasts such as in the incidents of the Samjhauta Express (February 2007), Mecca Masjid (May 2007) and Ajmer Sharief

(October 2007)? The cases filed against the Babri Masjid demolition accused move at an excruciatingly slow pace whereas little movement is seen on the suspects who carried out the anti-Muslim carnages in Mumbai and elsewhere. In Gujarat, investigation/prosecution into the anti-Muslim carnage of 2002 began only because of a stubborn campaign by concerned social activists. Such is the official bias that the largest private militia in the country, Bajrang Dal and its various clones operate with impunity. They can rape, molest, bomb, plunder, abuse, blackmail and assault, all in the name of religion/cultural nationalism, and rarely feel the weight of law against them.

Moreover, if Mumbai attack stands out because of the fact that the armed gunmen happened to be Pakistanis, then where do we place the Samjhauta Express blast (February 2007) in which 64 out of 68 were Pakistanis, including six minors, killed on Indian soil? In the Samjhauta Express blast case, the Haryana police was convinced about involvement of groups like Lashkar-e-Taiba (LeT) and the Indian authorities formally asked Pakistan to search for a person whom the Haryana police investigators were looking for. After an initial flurry of activity and leaks about the leads, the trail turned cold. This is despite the fact that, in 2000, Hindu fascists had threatened to disrupt train services between India and Pakistan. Also, two men whose sketches were released by Haryana police, according to witnesses, spoke Hindi. They had argued with the railway police when they were pulled up for entering the train without tickets, and had claimed that they wanted to go to Ahmedabad, but then got off the train just 15 minutes before the blast, as the train slowed down, for some inexplicable reason, just before Panipat. And yet, not once, during the entire investigation, or subsequently, when investigators got nowhere, did the police or the central agencies entertain the likely involvement of some Hindu fanatic group in the crime, that is, until the Malegaon 2008 probe began in earnest, and some leads pointed towards the likely involvement of Hindu fanatics. After the Mumbai attack, the probe into Samjhauta Express train blast, as well as the Mecca Masjid and Ajmer Sharief cases, has stalled. Why?

The point is not to deny the presence of fanatics among minorities in India or to whitewash the crimes of the Pakistan-based LeT, but to stress that in India the threat posed by Hindu fanatics multiplies many times over, because it enjoys the protection of the state. The prosecutors do not invoke treason and sedition laws against them as the Malegaon (2008) chargesheet reveals. Unlike India's minorities and underclass, Hindu fanatics never face the threat of proscription nor are they subjected to harsh procedures. Their horrible acts do not make them pariahs for the mainstream media; rather the latter goes out of its way to allow them time and space to explain themselves, a privilege rarely extended to minority groups such as Students Islamic Movement of India (SIMI) or even the underclass organizations such as Naxalites, or insurgents from Jammu and Kashmir (J&K) and the northeast. Is it that Hindus are considered mere 'overzealous nationalists'? How dissimilar is this from Pakistani claims that Muslim groups like the Taliban and the LeT are 'misguided patriots'?

Sweeping rhetoric, therefore, undercuts the Indian state's own credibility. Just as fact and fiction have been mixed up often by the Indian state and media, it is not surprising that Pakistan too acts in the same vein.

Root Causes

This brings me to the final point. The Mumbai attack points towards drawing a clear line between attacks linked to causes which are rooted inside the country, and those that are carried out by groups located outside, using these as a cover for their own myopic world view. It is perverse to argue that because the Indian state brutalizes people say in J&K, therefore, Pakistan-based LeT's mass murders flow from that action. Just as revolution cannot be exported neither can right to resist oppression become an exportable commodity. It is equally perverse to claim that, because Pakistan allows LeT to operate freely and carry out its vicious campaign against non-Muslims, therefore, Indian Muslims or visiting Pakistanis should be made to suffer, as Hindutva groups believe. People, who suffer brutalization at the hands of security forces, such as in J&K, have the inalienable right to offer resistance, but even they cannot target civilians. Unfortunately, it is one thing to espouse this, quite another matter for it to be followed. The reason is that those who are motivated by hatred will continue to practise what they preach and they clutch at excuses, which can keep shifting. It is thus that root causes behind internal conflicts and simmering discontent among sections of our own people get linked with such acts as the Mumbai attack. The LeT, which carried out the attack in Mumbai, in the e-mail sent under the name of Deccan Mujahedeen, justified the massacre in order to avenge injustices perpetrated on the Muslim community in India since 1947 (*The Indian Express*, 28 November 2009).

However much they offend our sensibilities, or however totally hypocritical such claims sound when made by mass murderers, the fact is that Indian society has suffered from gross injustices perpetrated against our own people. One of the most flagrant forms of these is the bias and prejudice practised by the state and its pavlovian recourse to military suppression when confronted by separatism or rebellion of the marginalized people. Consequently, the umbilical ties between the Indian state and the Hindutva groups have to be addressed and we must have the courage to search for democratic resolutions of internal conflicts. This is within the grasp of the Indian state and also its constitutional obligation. Providing speedy justice to the victims of all heinous crimes robs hate mongers and mass murderers of their raison d'être and blunts their capacity to mobilize support and inflict harm. Thus, for all the pain it has caused, the Mumbai attack ought to become an occasion for us to look inwards in order to rectify wrongs which exist. This does not require pleading for international support, use of coercive diplomacy, diversion of scarce resources at a time of economic meltdown, or feeling frustrated with Pakistan's dilatory tactics. We can neither control the external world nor choose our neighbours. But it is possible to secure our state and society, and influence the course of events in India and the world outside, by ensuring justice for our own people who are marginalized and suffer persecution.

Notes

1. Despite spending $25 billion after 1999 and committed to purchase military hardware worth $30 billion between 2007 and 2012, the Indian armed forces remain ill-prepared to launch an attack on Pakistan. There is enough material available in the public domain to know that, apart from US pressure, there were other pressing reasons that helped rule out war. A good analysis is offered by Manoj Joshi writing in *Mail Today* (17 January 2009) wherein he notes that the Indian armed forces were unwilling to 'guarantee' that a surgical strike would not spiral into an all-out war. He further pointed out that the stocks of ammunition, missiles and equipment, which is maintained for an offensive action, was found lacking. He also notes that '[t]he heavy involvement of the Army in counter-insurgency operations cannot but affect its preparedness for its primary role, which is to defend the country against external aggression'. In fact, it is interesting to note that counter-insurgency has resulted in poor performance of Indian army officers with only 23–25 per cent clearing the in-house-service exams for promotions. Retired Lt General H.S. Bagga, formerly director-general of the army's manpower, planning and personnel division, says that until the 'late 80s, when Kashmir was peaceful, almost 80 to 90% officers cleared these exams' (*The Hindustan Times*, 2 February 2009).
2. In the one-day debate in the Lok Sabha on 11 December 2008 on the amendments moved for UAPA as well as the National Investigation Agency, there were 50 members present in the morning; at 3.30 p.m. there were 78 members, which fell to 47 by 6 p.m. When the prime minister spoke there were only 90 members present. The effective strength of the house is 507 out of 552 seats earmarked by the Constitution.
3. It is also worth noting that against a sanctioned strength of 15.7 lakh state police, of which 1,209,904 was civil force and 314,122 was armed police in 2007, the shortfall was 118,005 in civil police and 50,000 in state armed police.

4. There is some confusion in the news report which mentions 127 additional battalions for the central paramilitary force, but the break-up provided adds up to 125 battalions, which is as follows: 10 for CRPF, 10 for ITBP, 27 for BSF, 37 for CISF, 37 for SSB and 4 for NSG (Jain, 28 January 2009).
5. The Report of the Group of Ministers on National Security entitled 'Reforming the National Security System' (February 2001) had suggested: 'In the long run, dispersal of the NSG units at strategic points across the country, would enhance its operational efficiency' (para 4.74, p. 52). Why was this recommendation not implemented? They had also recommended that the NSG 'should not be deployed for duties, which stretch far beyond its original mandate, as this results in enormous wastage of resources' (para 4.73). Surely VIP duty is one such wastage of public money. Moreover, it is the Indian public which needs protection from many a person being protected by NSG.
6. The GoM report was presented in February 2001 and therefore it is assumed that military expenditure after that took into account the requirements in line with the recommendations which were made. See also Navlakha (2006) for details.

References

Indian Express. 2008. 'In Hindi, this Terror Mail is Different', Express News Service, 28 November.

Jain, Bharti. 2009. 'Get Ready to March Past the Job Blues', *Economic Times*, 28 January.

Joshi, Manoj. 2009. 'Was the Army Ready for War?', *Mail Today*, 17 January.

Navlakha, Gautam. 2006. 'Shrinking Horizon of an Expanding Economy: India's Military Spending', *Economic and Political Weekly*, 41(14), 8 April: 1338–40.

Parashar, Sachin. 2007. 'IB, Cops in Murky Frameup', *The Times of India*, New Delhi, 13 September.

Reddy, U. Sudhakar. 2008. 'New Outfits May Have Links With Lashkar', *Asian Age*, New Delhi, 28 November.

Singh, Rahul. 2009. 'Most Army Officers Flunk Annual Exams', *Hindustan Times*, New Delhi, 2 February.

Epilogue

Six months down the line, the aftermath of Mumbai attack, what is most visible left over is in form of the trial of Ajmal Kasab, the sole terrorist who was caught alive by the brave policeman. The immediate reaction of the society has given way to a more reasoned form, the cry of attacking Pakistan; the anti-Pakistan sentiments have been muted.

Mumbai attack was a one of the most painful chapters of the city's life. After that episode, over a period of time, we note that the guns and bombs of terrorists are targeting Pakistan in a very serious way. A series of bomb blasts have shaken the Pakistan society. Pakistan President Asif Ali Zardari went to the extent of saying that Pakistan is the bigger victim of terror attacks than India. Partly he is right, as beginning from the assasination of Benazir Bhutto there had been regular terror attacks there. The thought process and common perception that Pakistan is the enemy country and is promoting terrorism in India has slightly got a different twist by now. Now it is obvious that within Pakistan itself there are diverse forces, which are working at cross purposes. The military–mullah complex though dislodged from power is not totally sidelined. Even the dreaded ISI has been targeted by a bomb blast (27 May 2009). The democratic Government of Pakistan has a different approach to the acts of terror which seems to be very clear by now. Also one knows the limitations of a democratically elected government. These limitations are due to the persistence of the influence of a powerful dominating army and conservative religious elements.

As neighbours grow together, as they have to live together, they also get affected by each others' problems. The only difference is that generally democratic governments are more trustworthy than the dictatorial regimes. The dictatorial regimes are the ones who rule with a heavy hand and have no answerability to the people. In India with the arrest of Sadhvi Pragya Singh Thakur and the whole lot of those involved in various bomb blasts, the cycle of terror seems to have been checked in a big way, society has got a reprieve, breathing time. It is also the time that the society, state and the government can mull over the issue and take the preventive steps rationally and firmly. With the Al Qaeda being engaged more seriously in Pakistan, its focus and nuisance value in India should go down over a period of time. The process of strengthening of democracy in Pakistan is the positive development in this region. It will not only benefit the people of Pakistan, but it also has the potential to change the political language of South Asia.

With the events which have taken place in last few months, a process of reformulation about terrorism is going in the social psyche. Various truths about the nasty phenomenon of terrorism can be understood more clearly now. That it is not related to religion or religious communities has been repeated *ad nauseum*, but the unfolding of current events has demonstrated the same in very clear terms. The tragic events of Pakistan and the halt, hopefully permanent or semi-permanent, of the terror attacks in India, give us message to look beyond the obvious to decipher the phenomenon to unravel the truth. Far too long the perceptions have shaped which relate this phenomenon to a particular religious community, teachings of a particular religion to the dreaded act. Events have demonstrated in the contemporary history that LTTE, the Sadhvi gang and Al Qaeda, all have done their nasty bit to aggravate the sufferings of society.

The regime change in the US should also have a peaceful impact in the region. Barrack Hussein Obama seems to have put brakes on the aggressive postures of US foreign policy. The biggest contribution of the new administration has been to convince Pakistan that it should not regard India as 'enemy number one'. The result has been the pressure of Pakistan army on Indian border has come down. Large battalions of Pakistan are being shifted from the Indian border to deal with the menace of Taliban. It should have a positive impact on India–Pakistan relations leading to intensification of peace processes within these countries.

The realization that terrorism itself is a multi-factorial phenomenon will help a lot in the overall combating of the issue. One should hope that Pakistani army takes up the resolve to eliminate Al Qaeda a bit more seriously and one hopes that it succeeds in its mission. That will be a turning point in this area; it will bring a serious halt to what has been referred as cross-border terrorism.

One of the crucial points to be noted in this context is the fatwa by Darool Uloom Deoband, the largest Islamic seminary in India. This seminary called a huge meeting of maulanas and issued a fatwa, stating that in acts of terrorism, innocent people get killed. Killing of innocent people is against the teachings of Islam and so terrorism has no sanction in Islam.

It is apparent that the better coordination of government agencies, the control of Al Qaeda–Taliban by Pakistan army will definitely create an atmosphere where terrorism would come under control and the massive tragedies resulting from that would come to an end.

Appendix I
Acts of Terrorism by RSS Combine

While currently the total focus of investigating agencies is to identify acts of terror with Muslim groups and Muslim youth, a very serious omission is taking place. This is due to the conceptual inadequacy of the state machinery or due to motives which are beyond the comprehension of large sections of communities and the activists engaged in issues related to violation of rights of minorities.

1. On 6 April 2006 two Bajrang Dal workers died when making the bombs. The place where they died belonged to the RSS worker and saffron flag was hoisted atop the hose. There was also a board of Bajrang Dal Nanded Branch on the wall of the house.

    Police recovered the materials for making IED devices, a diary and fake beard, moustache and Pajama Kurta. The Anti Terrorist Squad established that the place was used for making bombs. The house search revealed the powerful bomb, IED with timer and remote control, after which the Inspector General of police conceded that it was a bomb blast and that those involved in the blast are the members of Bajrang Dal. Local papers reported that a diary has the details of bomb-making techniques and other relevant information.

    On 11 April, Special IG Police Mr Surya Prakash Gupta declared that it was not an isolated event;

rather a bomb-manufacturing centre (Bomb Nirmiti Kendra) was functional at the house of Rajkondwar. He said this centre was working since many days. He said one of the injured, Rahul Pande, had categorically confessed to have made many such bombs earlier.

Incidents of bomb blasts were witnessed in many places around that time, Parbhani, Jalna and Aurangabad in Maharashtra. Most of these were in front of the mosques. The Nanded investigation 'leads' were not pursued. The attitude of police in this investigation has been totally lax. Social activists made the complaint about this to Human Rights Commission.

Beyond the geographical similarities, the details of the attacks which took place in the nearby areas were uncanny: each took place between 1:45 and 2:00 in the afternoon, just after Friday prayers, at the most prominent mosque in town. The bomb that went off in Nanded in 2006 on 6 April, a Thursday, was apparently meant to be set off at an Aurangabad masjid the following day.

In same Nanded, on 10 February 2007, 28-year-old Pandurang Bhagwan Amilkanthwar died on the spot. 'Amol Biscuits', a bakery shop, was run by the deceased, at Shastrinagar, Nanded. Shop was closed from outside. He was a Shiv Sena Shakha *pramukh*.

2. In Thane on 4 June 2008, two Hindu Jagran Samiti workers were arrested for planting the bombs in the basement of Gadkari Rangayatan, due to which seven people got injured. The same group was involved in the blasts in Vashi, Panvel also. This group idolizes Savarkar (Hindu Mahasabha) and Hedgewar (RSS) and indoctrinates its members into hating Christians and Muslims.

3. On 24 August 2008 two Bajrang Dal activists died in Kanpur while making bombs. The Kanpur zone IGP S.N. Singh stated that their investigations have revealed that this group was planning massive explosions all over the state.
4. *Indian Express*, 23 October 2008 reports that those involved in the bomb blast in Malegaon and Modasa (September 2008) had links with Akhil Bhartiya Vidyarthi Parishad.
5. In Goa, on 17 October 2009 in Margao a bomb went off killing two workers of Sanatana Sanstha.

Similarly in Tenkasi, Tamil Nadu pipe bomb attack on RSS office (January 2008) was projected to have been done by jihadi Muslims. The investigation revealed many a Hindu names and later the investigation was frozen. In an alleged Fidayin attack on RSS office in Nagpur (1 June 2006), it was claimed that three of them were killed in the police encounter, as per the police version. Citizens Inquiry report, headed by Justice Kolse Patil doubted the police version in a serious way; the clarifications did not come through from the authorities.

By now a pattern is emerging where not only that Bajrang Dal activists are carrying guns and swords in the public display of the arms but are also active in undertaking the acts of terror. It is likely that in many cases their role has remained uninvestigated. There is a deliberate cover up of these incidents. Some of these leads are not being pursued while the police are hyperactive in cases where suspected Muslims youth seem to be involved, and that too just on the basis of their confessions. This is a biased attitude of the authorities involved.

Appendix II

Unraveling Truth: People's Tribunal on Atrocities Committed in the Name of Combating Terrorism

Acts of terror have been a major menace for the society during last few years. Starting from the post-Mumbai riot bomb blasts till the latest ones in Ahmedabad, these have been terrifying the society in a dangerous way. Following the 9/11 in 2001 and propagation of the word 'Islamic terrorism' by US media, 'all terrorists are Muslims' has become a part of social common sense.

The major victims of these acts of terror are not only those who get killed or wounded in the blasts etc. But also those innocents who are caught hold of on the suspicions which have generally not been validated so far by further investigation. The life of blasts victims ruins them totally and the lives of those innocents caught by reckless attitude of police and condoned by judiciary are shattered beyond repair. This is what emerged from the interim observations of the Jury of People's Tribunal on the Atrocities Committed against Minorities in the name of fighting terrorism, organized by ANHAD, Human Rights Law Network and Peace (Hyderabad, 22–24 August 2008).

The jury included eminent judges, legal luminary, senior journalists, academics and social workers, Justice S.N. Bhargava (retired Chief Justice, Sikkim High Court),

Justice Sardar Ali Khan, retired High Court Judge, Asghar Ali Engineer; Islamic scholar, K.G. Kannabiran (National President, PUCL), Prashant Bhushan, Advocate Supreme Court, Ram Puniyani (former professor IIT, Mumbai), Professor Rooprekha Verma (retired Vice Chancellor, Lucknow University), Kingsukh Nag, Editor *Times of India* and Lalit Surjan, Editor *Deshbandhu*, Raipur. In addition rights activist Kavita Shrivastava recounted her experiences of police attitude in the wake of Jaipur blasts, Suresh Khairnar narrated the findings of his committee for investigation of Nanded blasts and alleged attack on RSS head office in Nagpur and Tehelka journalist Ajit Sahi narrated the myths and facts about SIMI. It emerged that a lot of allegations about this organization are totally unsubstantiated.

There were scores of depositions, recounting pain and tragedy. The legal luminaries cross examined them to ensure that truth comes out. There were lot of similarities in the pattern of testimonies despite diverse type of cases and regions. The stories of innocence of most of the accused were transparent. The attitude of police and judiciary appeared to be uniformly biased. The ruining of lives of many of the victims and their families was heart rending and audience and the jury were moved in most cases.

The police bias are glaringly obvious, the line of investigation is neither professional nor objective. One notes that observations where the definitive evidence is definitive have been totally bypassed while strategizing investigations. In Nanded two Bajrang Dal workers died while making bombs (April 2006); in Kanpur (August 2008) also similarly two of them died and in Thane the members of Hindu Jagran Samiti were involved without any shadow of doubt. Why have these leads been suppressed by authorities is the question the political leadership should answer.

Some of the testimonies are very revealing. Yakub Khan from Coimbatore was arrested in the wake of 1998 blasts, accused of being a member of a terrorist outfit about which he had never heard and was tortured. Ten years down the line no charges were proved and he was released with 10 precious years of his life lost and his career as a student of professional college totally ruined. His friend Shiv Kumar, converted to Islam as Abdul Hamid, was arrested in the same way and in addition was told that he would not have been arrested had he not converted to Islam.

Shabbir Masiulllah Ansari was actually in police custody when the Malegaon blasts took place, but he languishes in jail for those charges. Maulana Muhammad Zahid has been implicated in the Malegaon blast, when actually he was 500 kilometres away in Phulsavangi, a place where he conducts *namaz* in the mosque. Many a bread winners of the families have been implicated worsening the economic plight of those families.

Most of the testimonies, well supported by various documents, were submitted to the tribunal. While the final report is being worked out, it became apparent that most of the time police is clueless about the culprits, is gripped by the biases. They catch hold of Muslim youth on suspicions which do not have much basis. This is happening at various places but more so in Maharashtra, Gujarat, Madhya Pradesh, Andhra Pradesh and Rajasthan. The communalization of police apparatus and their high-handed methods have no legality; the protectors of the law seem to be the biggest violators of law, as the tribunal in its interim observations points out, 'In most of the cases, the persons picked up are not shown to be arrested by the police until many days after their arrest in gross violation of the law. Their families are also not informed about their arrest. In many cases, they have been tortured in police custody and made to "confess" and sign blank papers. The police has been often humiliating Muslim detainees on the ground of their religion. The testimonies show widespread communalization of the police across states in the country.'

The communal bias of police gets a full backing from the judiciary as they grant the remand even without any concrete evidence against the suspect. One also observes that the major 'evidence', the 'cracking' of cases, is based on the confessions, which are extracted in the police custody, under all unspeakable tortures, electric shocks and pouring of acid on private parts. It must be giving the police officials a sadistic pleasure apart from helping them to frame the alleged culprits and pat their backs for solving the cases. A section of media does the rest of the job, sensationalizing the episodes, no critical examination of the version of the police! Media, which is supposed to be the watch dog, at most of the times, supplements the role of state in 'manufacturing' the evidence against the hapless innocent alleged culprits.

One of the major concerns shown by the tribunal is that not only this traumatizes and brutalizes a section of community; it may be letting the real culprits get away with their game. So far despite so many blasts, the only times where the definitive evidence has been found are the ones related to Nanded, Kanpur (Bajrang Dal) and Thane–Vashi (Hindu Jagran Samiti). SIMI has emerged as the favourite culprit for police, surely it is not above suspicion, but still the definitive evidence is nowhere in sight.

The tribunal has made many interim recommendations; the hope is that the civic society and sensitive media's pressure will make the authorities listen to the voice of reason and pain of the victims of 'investigation mismanagement'. The Human Rights and Minorities commissions must take up these violations by the police, suo motu, should act as a check on the excesses of police. The judiciary must ensure that there are genuine grounds for police custody, and that human rights of suspects are respected. There should be special trial courts for such cases, with medical person available to check the torture inflicted on the victims; those implicated wrongly must be compensated and when necessary the guilty police officers should be made to pay the compensation. Media should restrain from publicizing mere allegations, narco analysis should not be abused, explicit permission of alleged culprits, for the same should be a must, and police reforms must be implemented to ensure that police respect the dignity of those arrested.

The work of the tribunal is significant and a timely intervention in the political scenario but its relevance will depend on many political and social factors. The deeper need for a movement to uphold the methods of law, protection of human rights of weak is a must today.

Select Bibliography

References

Ahmad, Ajiaz. 2004a. *On Communalism & Globalization: Offensives of the Far Right (Three Essays* Press). New Delhi.

———. 2004b. *Iraq, Afghanistan & the Imperialism of Our Time.* Delhi: Left Word Books.

Ali, Tariq. 2002. *The Clash of Fundamentalism: Crusades, Jihads & Modernity.* Delhi: Rupa & Co.

Armstrong, Karen. 2000. *Islam: A Short History.* London: Phoenix Press.

Imam, Zafar. 2004. *Iraq-2003: The Return of Imperialism.* Delhi: Aakar Books.

Koshy, Ninan. 2002. *War on Terror; Reordering the World.* Delhi: Left Word Books.

Maley, William. 2001. *Afghanistan & the Taliban: The Rebirth of Fundamentalism?* Delhi: Penguin Books India.

Mamdani, Mahmood. 2003. *Good Muslim Bad Muslim.* Hyderabad: Orient Longman.

Prashad, Vijay. 2002. *War against the Planet: The Fifth Afghan War, Imperialism, & Other Assorted Fundamentalisms.* Delhi: Left Word Books.

Puniyani, Ram. 2002. *Terrorism Imperialism & War.* Mumbai: BUILD.

———. 2006. *Terrorism, Facts Versus Myth.* Delhi: Pharos Media.

Said, Edward W. 2000. *The End of the Peace Process: Oslo & After.* New York: Vintage Books.

Further Readings

1. 'Congressman: US Set Up Anti-Taliban to be Slaughtered'. This is an account of how the US covertly supported the Taliban. This is available at http://emperors-clothes.com/misc/rohr.htm

2. 'Washington's Backing of Afghan Terrorists: Deliberate Policy'. Article from *Washington Post* with introductory note from 'Emperor's Clothes'. Can be read at http://emperors-clothes.com/docs/anatomy.htm
3. 'Taliban Camps US bombed in Afghanistan Were Built by NATO'. Documentation from the *New York Times*. Combined US and Saudi aid to Afghan-based terrorism totaled $6 billion or more. Can be read at http://emperors-clothes.com/docs/camps.htm
4. 'CIA Worked with Pakistan to Create Taliban'. From *Times of India*. Can be read at http://emperors-clothes.com/docs/pak.htm
5. 'Osama bin Laden: Made in USA'. Excerpt from article on US bombing of a pill factory in Sudan in August 1998. Argues that bin Laden was, and still may be, a CIA asset. Can be read at http://emperors-clothes.com/articles/jared/madein.htm
6. Excerpts from News Reports: 'Bin Laden in the Balkans' Evidence that bin Laden aided or is aiding the U.S.-sponsored forces in Bosnia, Kosovo and Macedonia. Can be read at http://emperors-clothes.com/news/binl.htm
7. 'The Creation Called Osama', by Shamsul Islam can be read at http://emperors-clothes.com/analysis/creat.htm; http://emperors-clothes.com/news/abc.htm

Websites

www.sacw.net
www.countercurrents.org
www.sabrang.com
www.csss-isla.com
www.anhadinfo.com
www.pluralindia.com

About the Editors and Contributors

The Editors

Ram Puniyani was a Professor at IIT Mumbai from 1984 to 2004. He was associated with the work of national integration and communal harmony from 1993. Part of the campaigns were associated with secular initiatives. He has contributed regular articles/essays on the topic, and has conducted workshops on the theme of national integration. He has been awarded Indira Gandhi National Integration Award (2006), and National Communal Harmony Award (2007). He has written books like *Communalism Facts versus Myths* (2003), *Religion Power and Violence* (2005), *Contours of Hindu Rashtra* (2006), *Terrorism Facts versus Myths* (2006), *Second Assasination of Gandhi* (2004).

Shabnam Hashmi is a social activist, a rebel, a fearless fighter and a human rights defender. She has been working as a social activist, and in 2003 formed Anhad. She was nominated for the Nobel Peace Prize as part of the 1000 women from across the world in 2005. She was awarded the Association for Communal Harmony in Asia (ACHA) Star Award for Communal Harmony in 2005, Smriti Samman in 2005 and the National Minority Rights Award 2008 by the National Minority Commission. She is a member of the National Integration Council, Ministry of

Home Affairs, Government of India, a Council Member of the National Literary Mission, Ministry of Human Resource Development, Govt. of India.

The Contributors

K.G. Balakrishnan is the 37th Chief Justice of India. He is the only dalit to become the Chief Justice of India till date.

Prashant Bhushan is a public interest lawyer in the Supreme Court.

Praful Bidwai is an Indian journalist, political analyst and activist.

Colin Gonsalves is the Executive Director of the Human Rights Law Network and a pioneer in public interest law in India.

Raveena Hansa is an independent journalist and columnist.

Biju Mathew is an Assistant Professor of Information Systems at Raider University.

Gautam Navlakha is an editorial consultant with EPW and member of one of India's oldest non-funded civil liberties group based in Delhi, namely People's Union for Democratic Rights.

Anand Patwardhan is an Indian documentary film-maker, known for his activism through social action documentaries on topics ranging from corruption, slum dwellers, nuclear arms race and citizen activism to communalism.

P. Sainath, the 2007 winner of the Ramon Magsaysay award for journalism, literature, and creative communication arts, is an Indian development journalist. He is the Rural Affairs editor of *The Hindu*.

Gnani Sankaran is a popular writer in the Tamil language. He has also written articles under the pseudonyms Vamban, Cynic and Nandan and is known for frank and uncompromising views on politics and culture, which he has expressed in the media for 30 years.

Sukla Sen is a well-known social activist attached to EKTA (Committee for Communal Amity), Mumbai.

Yoginder Sikand is the author of several books on Islam-related issues in India. He is the editor and primary writer of *Qalandar*, a monthly electronic publication covering relations between Muslims and followers of other religions.

Tarun Tejpal has been an editor with the *India Today* and the *Indian Express* groups, and the managing editor of *Outlook*. He is the founder of *Tehelka*—which has garnered international fame for its aggressive public interest journalism. In 2001, *Asia Week* listed Tejpal as one of Asia's 50 most powerful communicators, and *Business Week* declared him among 50 leaders at the forefront of change in Asia. Tarun's debut novel, *The Alchemy of Desire*, was hailed by the *Sunday Times* as 'an impressive and memorable debut', and by *Le Figaro* as a 'masterpiece'. In 2007 *The Guardian*, UK, named Tarun Tejpal among the 20 who constitute India's newslite.